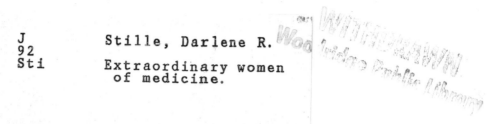

EXTRAORDINARY

WOMEN OF

MEDICINE

by

DARLENE R. STILLE

Children's Press®
A Division of Grolier Publishing
New York London Hong Kong Sydney
Danbury, Connecticut

Acknowledgments
The editors would like to thank Bernadine Healy, Elisabeth Kübler-Ross, Antonia Novello, and June Osborn for their kind and generous assistance in compiling their biographical information for this book.

Library of Congress Cataloging-in-Publication Data
Stille, Darlene R.
Extraordinary women of medicine / by Darlene R. Stille
p. cm. — (Extraordinary people)
Includes bibliographical references and index
Summary: Presents biographical sketches highlighting the contributions of women, mostly American, to the field of medicine in the nineteenth and twentieth centuries.
ISBN 0-516-20307-X (lib. bdg.)   0-516-26145-2 (pbk.)
1. Women physicians—Biography—Juvenile literature. 2. Women medical scientists—Biography—Juvenile literature. 3. Women in medicine—History—Juvenile literature.
[1. Women in medicine. 2. Physicians. 3. Women—Biography.] I. Title. II. Series.
R692.S75 1997
610′92′2—dc20
[B]
                                                                                    96-43196
                                                                                         CIP
                                                                                          AC

Contents

 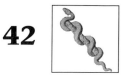

65

THE FIRST
AFRICAN-AMERICAN
WOMEN DOCTORS

80

EMILY JENNINGS STOWE
1831–1903

*First Woman Licensed to
Practice Medicine in Canada*

99

SOPHIA JEX-BLAKE
1840–1912

*Pioneer in British Women's
Medical Education*

67

EMELINE HORTON CLEVELAND
1829–1878

*First Woman Doctor to
Perform Major Surgery*

83

MARY EDWARD WALKER
1832–1919

*First Woman
U.S. Army Surgeon*

104

MARY PUTNAM JACOBI
1842–1906

*Leader in the Study
of Women's Health*

71

MARY HARRIS THOMPSON
1829–1895

*Founder of Women's
Hospital and Medical School*

88

CLARA A. SWAIN
1834–1910

*Pioneering Medical
Missionary*

110

MARY ELIZA MAHONEY
1845–1926

*First African-American
Graduate Nurse*

76

MARIE ELIZABETH ZAKRZEWSKA
1829–1902

*Founder of the New England
Hospital for Women and Children*

92

ELIZABETH GARRETT ANDERSON
1836–1917

*First British
Woman Doctor*

114

MARIE JOSEPHA MERGLER
1851–1901

*Renowned
Woman Surgeon*

117

SISTER MARY JOSEPH DEMPSEY
1856–1939
*Head of St. Mary's Hospital,
Rochester, Minnesota*

137

ANITA NEWCOMB MCGEE
1864–1940
*Founded the U.S. Army
Nurse Corps*

158

LILLIAN D. WALD
1867–1940
*Founder of Public
Health Nursing*

122

JANE ARMINDA DELANO
1862–1919
*Organized the Red Cross
Nursing Service*

142

SUSAN LAFLESCHE PICOTTE
1865–1915
*First Native-American
Woman Doctor*

162

MAUDE ELIZABETH SEYMOUR ABBOTT
1869–1940
*Pioneer in the Study of
Congenital Heart Defects*

126

BERTHA VAN HOOSEN
1863–1952
*Founder of the American
Medical Women's Association*

147

ANNIE W. GOODRICH
1866–1954
*First Dean of Yale University
School of Nursing*

166

ALICE HAMILTON
1869–1970
*Founder of Industrial
Medicine*

132

ELSIE INGLIS
1864–1917
*Heroic Surgeon
in World War I*

151

THE GOLDEN AGE
OF WOMEN DOCTORS

173

ESTHER POHL LOVEJOY
1869–1967
*Leader of American Women's
Hospitals Overseas*

177

MARIA MONTESSORI
1870–1952
*Famed Physician
and Educator*

194

Margaret Sanger
1879–1966
*Founder of the American
Birth Control Movement*

212

KAREN DANIELSEN HORNEY
1885–1952
Pioneering Psychiatrist

181

S. JOSEPHINE BAKER
1873–1945
*Pioneer in
Well-Baby Care*

199

ELIZABETH KENNY
1880–1952
*Developed Treatment
for Polio*

216

ANNA FREUD
1895–1982
*Pioneering Child
Psychoanalyst*

186

LILLIE ROSA MINOKA-HILL
1876–1952
*Beloved Native-American
Physician*

204

GLADYS ROWENA DICK
1881–1963
*Discovered Cause of
Scarlet Fever*

220

HELEN B. TAUSSIG
1898–1986
*Co-Developer of
"Blue-Baby" Operation*

190

ELSIE STRANG L'ESPERANCE
1878?–1959
*Founder of Cancer
Prevention Clinics*

208

FLORENCE A. BLANCHFIELD
1884–1971
*Superintendent of U.S. Army
Nurse Corps During World War II*

227

HATTIE ELIZABETH ALEXANDER
1901–1968
*Pioneer in the Diagnosis and
Treatment of Meningitis*

Women Healers in Ancient Times

Before the dawn of history, medicine was probably women's work. Many archaeologists and anthropologists believe that women were the first healers.

We can imagine a tribe of people living in caves and other crude shelters, going out to hunt animals or gather roots and berries for food. This is how prehistoric people spent most of their time—looking for food. The hunters were usually men and boys, because males have greater physical strength. Women were more likely to gather edible plants.

Over many centuries, as they learned which plants were good to eat, the women also learned that some were good for treating sickness. They found that chewing the bark of a certain tree or brewing a tea from a particular plant's leaves could help the symptoms of some diseases. In fact, many modern drugs come from plants. The bark of the cinchona tree produces quinine, a drug for treating malaria. The foxglove plant yields a compound called digitalis, which is used for heart conditions.

When a prehistoric woman gave birth, she undoubtedly was helped and tended by other women. When children fell ill, they probably were treated and nursed by their mother or other women in the household. If an older male broke a limb or was wounded while hunting, the women of the household were there to treat the injuries. In this way, women probably served as the first physicians, surgeons, and nurses in prehistoric times, and they passed their medical wisdom on from one generation to the next.

The first historical record of medical treatment is almost five thousand years old and comes from ancient Egypt. The Egyptians recognized many diseases, from cancer to tuberculosis, developed drugs in the form of salves and potions, and even performed minor surgical operations. They recorded their medical knowledge on papyrus scrolls.

Women physicians practiced in ancient Egypt. Many of them specialized in obstetrics and gynecology. One of Egypt's great medical schools was located at the Temple of Saïs and was devoted to the training of women doctors. Because the causes of many diseases were beyond the understanding of people long ago, the early physicians relied on religion and magic as much as medicine for treatment and cures. Therefore, many medical schools and treatment centers were located in temples.

Western medicine, which relied more on reason than on magic, began in ancient Greece. The most famous Greek healers of legend are Asclepius, the Greek god of healing, his daughters Hygeia, who represented prevention, and Panacea, who represented cure. Temples of healing were dedicated to this Greek family, and the snake-entwined staff each member carried is still the symbol of medicine today.

Gradually, women were removed from the practice of medicine in Greece. By the fourth century B.C., women of Athens were forbidden to practice medicine. As a result, many women, reluctant to see male doctors, suffered needless deaths from complicated childbirths and gynecological problems. A Greek woman named Agnodice decided to remedy this by becoming a physician. She disguised herself as a man, attended medical school, and began practicing obstetrics and gynecology. She

Greek healer Asclepius

was very popular with her women patients. But one day, her disguise was uncovered by the male authorities and she was brought to trial for breaking the law. She could have been sentenced to death, but the women of Athens rose up in protest. Not only was Agnodice acquitted, but the law was changed and women were once again allowed to practice medicine.

Historians do not know much about the women healers of ancient Rome until the Christian era began. The most famous early Roman healer was a woman named Fabiola, who lived in the fourth century. She was born into a wealthy Roman family, but at age twenty, she converted to Christianity, and became a follower of St. Jerome. Fabiola dedicated her life to caring for the sick and destitute. She and her friend Paula are credited with founding the first public hospital in Europe.

The fall of the Roman Empire brought about the Dark Ages in Europe. During that time, the little medical learning and healing that existed was kept alive and per-

Hildegarde Bingen

formed in monasteries and convents. A famous woman musician, mystic, and writer on medicine named Hildegarde Bingen came from a convent in Germany. She was born in 1098 and lived more than eighty years. Because of her writings and miraculous cures, her fame spread throughout Europe.

As the Dark Ages ended, universities sprang up. The university at Salerno in Italy was home to the most famous woman physician of medieval times, Trotula. She was married to another famous doctor, and their sons also became physicians. Trotula was on the faculty of the university and specialized in gynecology and obstetrics. The textbook that she wrote on these subjects in the eleventh century was used for hundreds of years.

In Europe during late Middle Ages, church doctrine made life very difficult for women healers. Most of these women were midwives who treated patients with medicines made from plants. Because of their special knowledge, the women often were suspected of being in league with the devil. Historians believe that many women who practiced the healing arts during the Middle Ages came to tragic ends. They were condemned as witches and burned at the stake.

With the Renaissance, which began in the sixteenth and seventeenth centuries, modern science was born. By the 1700s, medicine had become a respectable profession, and men began to take over the role of midwife. At first, women midwives—and women patients—objected to the idea of "men midwives." But by the 1800s, assisting at births had become an accepted job of doctors. And all doctors by that time were men.

The tasks women could perform were reduced in many areas, not just medicine, as society came to regard women as delicate and not very bright creatures. According to popular belief, education of any kind would be harmful to women, and the study of medicine was unthinkable. Not until the women's movement began in the mid-1800s did women begin to practice medicine again.

James (Miranda) Barry

Woman Doctor in Male Disguise

1795–1865

When the inspector general of the British Army Medical Department would march about the field hospitals, his subordinates often snickered behind his back and called him unmanly. The little red-headed doctor was unable to grow a beard. And no wonder. Dr. James Barry was really Miranda Barry, a woman who had disguised herself as a man in order to become a British Army surgeon. Even though no one knew it, Dr. Barry was the first British woman doctor.

Little is known about the early life of James Barry. She might have been born in London in 1795 and originally named Miranda Stuart. Historians have found some evidence that she might have been the granddaughter of a Scottish earl. She could have been the illegitimate child of the earl's daughter and a member of the British royal family. One historian speculates that Miranda's mother, knowing there was no opportunity at that time for women, raised little Miranda as a boy. At any rate, Miranda apparently attended the University of Edinburgh disguised as a male and graduated with a Doctor of Medicine degree in 1812.

British Army records show that, dressed as a man, she became an army hospital assistant on July 5, 1813. She rose steadily through the ranks, becoming an assistant surgeon in 1815 after the Battle of Waterloo, surgeon major in 1827, deputy inspector general in 1851, and inspector general, the highest rank in the British Army medical service, in 1858.

During Dr. Barry's lifetime, the British Empire controlled colonies all over the world, and stationed soldiers in all of them. Dr. Barry spent most of her medical career with the colonial troops. She served on the island of Malta and in the Cape Colony (today called South Africa). She also was sent to Jamaica, Trinidad, St. Helena, Mauritius, and Canada.

In 1859, Dr. Barry retired from the army and lived the rest of her life in rented lodgings in London with a black manservant who had been with her for years. She died on July 25, 1865. An examination was held and, to the shock of the doctors, James Barry was revealed to be a woman.

Why did this woman spend her life in the army disguised as a man? Was it love of medicine? Or was it love for another army surgeon? The examination at her death revealed that she had at some time during her life given birth to a child. The mysteries surrounding the life of James Miranda Barry may never be solved.

Dorothea Lynde Dix

Mental Health Care Reformer

1802–1887

At the age of twelve, Dorothea Dix ran away from home. "Home" was a crude hut in the wilderness of what is now the state of Maine. She lived there in poverty, loneliness, and despair with her father—who had difficulty holding a job—her sickly mother, and two brothers. Dorothea wanted a better life. She wanted to get an education and do something important in the world. So she left home to live with her well-to-do grandmother in Boston. She did go to school and eventually she did do something of great importance. Dorothea Dix changed the way that mentally ill people were treated. She rescued them from cruelty and imprisonment and introduced health officials to the idea of humane care for the mentally retarded and for people with emotional disturbances.

Dorothea Dix was born on April 4, 1802, in the village of Hampden, Maine. (Maine was then a part of Massachusetts.) She was the first child of Joseph and Mary Dix, a young couple with many economic and emotional burdens. Joseph, the son of Dr. Elijah Dix, a wealthy Boston physician and land developer, had been sent to study at Harvard University. Joseph's father had great plans for the young man's future. But Joseph fell in love with Mary Bigelow, a woman eighteen years older than he was. She apparently was uneducated and emotionally unstable. Much to his parents' dismay, Joseph dropped out of Harvard and married Mary.

Dr. Dix then sent the young couple off to some land he owned in the wilderness. Joseph was to manage these properties in Maine. But Joseph did not have a talent for business. Instead, he became a wandering preacher, and he also began to drink heavily. He had Dorothea write and produce religious pamphlets for him to hand out, and he then would leave for weeks or months, traveling around the countryside, preaching.

Dorothea's mother was not emotionally able to cope with her family on her own. Soon, Dorothea had two younger brothers, and the care of these brothers became Dorothea's job. Family life to young Dorothea must have seemed like a hopeless trap of poverty, emotional instability, and endless household chores.

Dorothea knew there was much more to life. Fortunately, she had visited her grandparents in Boston several times. The visits stopped after her grandfather died, when Dorothea was seven years old. But on those visits, Dorothea came to understand that there was a larger world of learning and culture beyond the grinding poverty of her frontier home. When she was twelve, Dorothea ran away. For the rest of her life, she would seldom talk about her childhood and never about how she came to flee Maine for life in Boston.

She lived first with her grandmother in Boston, then with other relatives in Worcester, Massachusetts. She was an enthusiastic student, and by the time she entered her teens, people were saying that she would make a good teacher, one of the accepted professions for women. At the age of fourteen, she opened a school for small children and taught there for three years before returning to Boston to further her own education. Eventually, she opened a school for young ladies in her grandmother's house.

During this time, Dorothea Dix had grown to be a tall and attractive woman, but "school marms" were supposed to be stern and plain-looking. So Dix began to dress plainly and behave sternly, and that was the image she presented to the world for the rest of her life.

Dorothea became fascinated with science and wrote a popular textbook, *Conversations on Common Things,* about the wonders of the natural world. She also became more deeply religious and joined the Unitarian Church. It was her religious convictions that led her toward the great work of her life—reforming the care of the mentally ill.

An odd set of circumstances guided her in that direction. First, she started a second school, a charity school for poor children. However, the strain of trying to run two schools made her ill—too ill to teach. A common treatment for mental and physical exhaustion in that day was to take a trip abroad, and that is what Dorothea did. She stayed in England with wealthy friends of her Unitarian pastor, and they introduced her to some fascinating people. One of them was Samuel Tuke, who had built a hospital for mental patients. Tuke believed that mental patients should be treated kindly and be given music to listen to and books to read. This approach was in marked contrast to the way mental patients usually were treated. Most of them were kept in prisons with criminals, chained, left in filthy, unheated cells, and barely given enough to eat.

However, Dix did not take on the cause of the mentally ill until several years after returning to Boston. Her grandmother had died, leaving Dorothea enough money on which to live. Dix led a somewhat aimless life until one fateful day, when she was asked to conduct a Sunday-school class for women prisoners at a local jail. At the jail, Dix found not only women convicted of crimes; she saw pitiful women in filthy rags, shivering with the cold in unheated cells. And what was their crime? They were mentally ill. Dix was outraged. The jailer protested that "lunatics" could not feel the cold. This viewpoint had many supporters among the general public.

Dix had found her life's work. At that time, there were no such professions as psychology or psychiatry. Dix pioneered in areas that would one day be covered by these fields. She began to study new ideas about treatment and new methods of providing institutions for the mentally ill. Then she undertook surveys of jails and poorhouses in Massachusetts and other states. Everywhere she found that mental patients were mistreated, even tortured. She documented what she found. Her first report was presented to the Massachusetts state legislature. "Gentlemen of Massachusetts," it read, "I have come to present to you the strong claims of suffering humanity. I come as the advocate of the helpless, forgotten, insane men and women held in cages, closets, cellars, stalls, pens; chained, naked, beaten with rods, and lashed into obedience. . . ."

She was painfully shy and never made public speeches. Instead, she enlisted powerful men in public life to present her reports. At first, she was ridiculed. But one by one, beginning with Massachusetts, she persuaded the states to pass laws, set aside funds, and build hospitals for the humane care of the mentally ill. In New Jersey, she fought a bitter but successful campaign in 1844 and 1845 to establish that state's first mental hospital at Trenton.

During the next three years, she traveled some 30,000 miles (50,000 kms.) investigating mental-patient treatment in a number of states, from Alabama to Pennsylvania, and Ohio to Illinois. The name of Dorothea Dix became a household word in the mid-1800s, and people came to accept her views. Instead of being ridiculed, her advice was sought by government officials. Railroads and steamboat companies gave her free travel passes.

Her focus then broadened from the state to the national level. She proposed establishing a national land trust to generate income that would be used to provide for care of the mentally ill. After many years, the plan was passed by Congress but vetoed by the president. Dix was crushed by this defeat and again went abroad to recover from exhaustion.

Instead of just resting, she began investigating treatment of mental patients in Scotland, France, Turkey, and Russia. She even wrung from the Pope a pledge to help improve conditions for Italy's mentally ill.

Back in America, Civil War erupted in 1861. Dix, now fifty-nine, volunteered to serve. She was appointed superintendent of nurses for the Union army. She selected the women nurses and set up programs to train them. She also established field hospitals wherever she could—in schools, churches, warehouses, even private homes. And she insisted on high standards of efficiency and cleanliness in caring for the sick and wounded soldiers.

The stress of her wartime duties began to take its toll on the frail and aging woman. Her demanding manner frequently brought her into conflict with military officers and other medical staff. But she remained in her post as head of nurses until the end of the Civil War, when she went back to her efforts at reforming mental-patient care.

When she was eighty years old, Dorothea Dix retired to an apartment at the Trenton hospital that she had established. She lived there until her death on July 17, 1887.

Ann Preston

*Pioneer in
Women's Medical
Education*

1813–1872

The male doctors of Philadelphia rose up in outrage; the local medical societies and the governing boards of Philadelphia's hospitals were united in their resolve. The idea of trying to educate women as doctors was absurd, and the upstart school trying to do so had to be shut down. The Woman's Medical College of Pennsylvania probably would have closed soon after it opened in 1850 had it not been for a tall, serene, and very practical Quaker woman named Ann Preston. By sheer determination, Dr. Preston was able not only to keep the little school alive, but to add a hospital and a nursing school, and to help build the Woman's Medical College into a major institution that into the twentieth century graduated thousands of women doctors.

Ann Preston was born on December 1, 1813, in the Quaker village of West Grove, Pennsylvania. The Preston family were abolitionists and strong believers in women's rights, so there were no intellectual or emotional blocks preventing young Ann from getting the education for which she longed.

After attending the local Quaker school, Ann went off to a boarding school in Chester, Pennsylvania. Soon she was called home, because her mother had fallen ill. Her mother never was well again, and as the oldest daughter in a family of nine children, Ann had to take over the household and help raise her younger brothers. She had no time for formal schooling, but she continued to educate herself by learning Latin and reading everything she could find on physiology and hygiene. She also was very active in the antislavery movement, even helping a runaway slave escape by the underground railway. And she worked in the temperance movement, which sought to forbid the sale of liquor.

West Grove was an intellectual as well as a religious center, so Ann Preston had the opportunity to hear lectures by some of the leading thinkers on women's rights, including Lucy Stone, Elizabeth Cady Stanton, and Susan B. Anthony. In addition, since girlhood Ann Preston had been friends with Lucretia Mott, another young Quaker woman who was to play an important role in the women's movement.

Preston saw a very practical need for women doctors. She had watched her two sisters and her mother die, she had seen other women endure one difficult pregnancy after another, and none of these women had adequate care, because the 1800s in America was an age of extreme modesty. Society pretended that women did not have bodies. Preston came to the conclusion that women patients would respond better to female doctors, who not only could treat them, but could also give them practical information about how to take care of their bodies.

When her brothers were grown and she was free to resume her education, Ann decided to become a doctor, even though at that time medical schools did not admit women. Her friends among the Quakers and women's rights activists gave her wholehearted encouragement. In 1847, she became a medical apprentice to a sympathetic Philadelphia doctor. After completing her two-year apprenticeship, Preston applied to the best medical schools in Philadelphia. They all turned her down because she was a woman.

Then she learned of the opening of a new school dedicated to educating women doctors—the Female (later renamed Woman's) Medical College of Pennsylvania. When the first class of seven students entered in 1850, Ann Preston was among them, and she never left the school again. After receiving an M.D. in December 1851, she stayed on for a year of post-graduate study. In 1853, she was appointed professor of physiology and hygiene.

Despite some local opposition, things went fairly well until 1858. That year, the Philadelphia County Medical Society denounced the school and recommended that local doctors and hospitals have nothing to do with its students. The next year, the state medical society passed a resolution condemning the Female Medical College as "irregular," engaging in the teaching of homeopathy and water cures and other unusual forms of treatment. Even though the school was quite "regular" in its teaching, the condemnations meant that the women students could not gain any practical experience at Philadelphia hospitals.

Dr. Preston's response was to plan a woman's hospital connected with the school. She called upon her Quaker friends to help raise funds, and sent a promising graduate, Emeline Horton Cleveland, to Paris, to learn the latest obstetrical and surgical techniques. The outbreak of the Civil War in 1861 forced the medical school to close for a time, but it reopened in 1862. The next year, Dr. Preston started a training school there for nurses. And in 1866, Dr. Preston was named the first woman dean of the Woman's Medical College of Pennsylvania.

Soon after becoming dean, Dr. Preston asked the state and county medical societies to repeal their ban on students and graduates of the women's school. The state medical society responded with another condemnation of women in the medical profession, saying that women were too delicate—mentally, physically, and emotionally—for such work and belonged in the home caring for their husbands and children. Dr. Preston wrote an eloquent reply that was printed in the May 4, 1867 issue of the *Medical and Surgical Reporter:*

"As responsible beings who must abide by the consequences of our course for time and for eternity we have decided for ourselves that the study and practice of medicine are proper, womanly and adapted to our mental, moral and physical constitution. . . . We feel, and society feels, that we are not usurping the place of men, but taking a position in the broad field of medicine which appropriately belongs to women; and that we shall enlarge the sphere of professional usefulness and contribute to the knowledge which shall bless the [human] race. . . ."

Despite the opposition, the women medical students did begin to gain admittance to the clinical lectures at the public hospitals. In 1868, Dr. Preston successfully applied to have her students accepted at the Pennsylvania Hospital clinic. However, unruly male students held a demonstration when the women students first tried to attend. This caused a scandal in Philadelphia, and public opinion was generally in favor of the women. Nevertheless, male professors and physicians sent out a document protesting the indelicacy and questionable morals of women who would be physicians. Dr. Preston replied in a newspaper article, "We maintain, in common with medical men, that science is impersonal and that the high aim of relief to suffering humanity sanctifies all duties." She further wrote, "Wherever it is proper to introduce women as patients, there also it is but just and in accordance with the instincts of the truest womanhood for women to appear as physicians and students."

The struggle took a toll on Dr. Preston's health, and she died at the age of fifty-eight on April 18, 1872. To the Woman's Medical College she left her books, medical instruments, and $4,000 to endow a scholarship. To the future women students she left proof that the pen was just as mighty as the scalpel in securing a place for women in the American medical profession.

Hannah E. Myers Longshore

---

*First Woman
Faculty Member at
an American
Medical School*

1819–1901

The whole Myers family shared in the chores on their farm near the Quaker colony of New Lisbon, Ohio. There was plenty of work to do on a farm in the early 1800s. Yet, every day, Hannah's parents, her four sisters, two step-sisters, and two brothers would gather for a family discussion. The topic might be religion or politics, the strategy for abolishing slavery, or an argument in favor of the rights of women. Hannah's family and most of her friends were Quakers, members of the Society of Friends, known for their humanitarian activities and their concern with education. Eventually, Hannah, some of her family members, and Quaker friends in Pennsylvania were involved in founding the world's first chartered medical school for women—the Woman's Medical College of Pennsylvania. Hannah was in the first graduating class. Even before being awarded her M.D., she was assisting in teaching, thus becoming the first woman faculty member at an American medical school.

Hannah E. Myers, born in Sandy Spring, Maryland, on May 30, 1819, was the first child of Samuel and Paulina Myers. Samuel, who taught at a Quaker school, had two daughters from a previous marriage. The family moved to Washington, D.C., and Hannah attended a Quaker school there. But many people in the District of Columbia were in favor of slavery, and Samuel and his family were very much opposed. To get away from this atmosphere, the Myerses moved to a farm in Ohio in 1833.

Education was important to Quaker families for boys and girls alike. Hannah attended school at the New Lisbon Academy, two miles (three kilometers) from the farm. She developed an interest in science and loved to observe and examine insects and small animals. When she still was quite young, she decided she would like to attend Oberlin College, a pioneering coeducational school, and then become a physician.

The Myers family was all in favor of Hannah's ambitions, but there were two major problems. The family had no money for college, and there were no medical schools that would admit women.

In 1841, Hannah married a teacher at the New Lisbon Academy, Thomas Ellwood Longshore. Thomas was a firm believer in the rights of women. Hannah still could not pursue her education, because she soon had two children to raise. As their family grew, so did Thomas's firm opposition to slavery. In fact, his antislavery views were considered so radical for that time that he lost his teaching job. Ironically, this personal misfortune would turn out to be very fortunate for Hannah and for the medical education of women.

With no means of support, in 1845 Thomas and Hannah packed up their belongings and their children and went back to his family in Bucks County, Pennsylvania, where Thomas found a teaching job at a local Quaker school. By this time, his brother, Joseph Skelton Longshore, had graduated from the University of Pennsylvania Medical School and was practicing as an eclectic physician. Eclectic physicians chose the best treatments from among the different competing approaches to medicine. At that time, treatment was merely guesswork, because the cause of disease was a complete mystery. "Regular" physicians favored bleeding or purging bad elements from the body, even though such harsh and ineffective treatment often made the patient worse, or even caused death. Therefore, many caring doctors looked for gentler methods of treatment.

Hannah told Joseph about her desire to become a physician, and he willingly agreed to have her study with him. Her sister-in-law, Anna Mary Longshore, also became apprenticed to Joseph. Becoming an apprentice was an accepted way of learning medicine until the later 1800s, when medical societies and associations were formed to raise the fairly low standards of medical education and practice.

Hannah and Mary read Joseph's books and observed him as he cared for patients. But Joseph knew that the women really needed to attend lectures and demonstrations at a medical school. In fact, some historians think that Hannah's enthusiasm and desire to learn medicine might have inspired Joseph to join with other Pennsylvania Quaker doctors and businessmen to establish the Female Medical College of Pennsylvania in 1850. Hannah Longshore enrolled in the first class and was one of the first eight graduates who received their M.D. degrees in December 1851.

Dr. Hannah Longshore began a private practice as Philadelphia's first woman doctor. Encouraged by such women's rights leaders as

Lucretia Mott, Dr. Longshore gave lectures on female sexual matters that shocked the local conservatives. But the lectures brought her patients, some even referred by doctors who publicly condemned her candid presentations. Hannah Longshore also served as an instructor in anatomy at the Female Medical College for about four years.

Then disagreement over how medicine should be taught caused a split among the faculty of the Female Medical College. Dr. Joseph Longshore, Dr. Hannah Longshore, and several others left to start a new eclectic medical school, the Penn Medical University, with both a male and a female department. Hannah Longshore became an anatomy instructor at Penn Medical, and her youngest sister and her half-sister both earned medical degrees there.

Hannah Longshore practiced medicine for about forty years. She treated the needy free of charge, and her family helped to collect food and clothing for them. At its peak, her practice extended to some three hundred families. Her own family and household grew, populated by friends and in-laws. It was always a center of lively discussions and a haven for those involved in social reform.

Dr. Longshore retired in 1892 and died on October 18, 1901, at her home in Philadelphia.

Florence Nightingale

Nurse

1820–1910

A girl born into upper-class English society during the Victorian Era of the 1800s could expect a carefree, idle life. She would spend her days sewing, drawing, and playing the piano. In the evenings she would enjoy parties, courtship, and eventually marriage with a well-to-do young man. But that life was not what Florence Nightingale wanted for herself. This young English lady was deeply troubled by the sickness and poverty she saw around her. At the age of sixteen, she felt called by God to do something about it. Against the protests of her family, she did. Her calling eventually led her to far-off Turkey to tend British soldiers wounded in war. They began calling her "The Lady of the Lamp" because at night she walked the dark hospital corridors, guided by a lamp, to comfort the wounded. She did much more than bring comfort—she also brought organization and efficient administration to the art of caring for the sick. For this, Nightingale is known today as the founder of the modern nursing profession.

Florence Nightingale was born on May 12, 1820, in the Italian city of Florence, where her wealthy parents were visiting and for which she was named. Her mother, Frances, and her father, William Edward, loved to travel. Their first daughter, Parthenope, had been born in Naples. At home in England, Florence and her sister grew up on their parents' country estates, where her father made sure Florence received a good education in languages and philosophy. Her mother was concerned with developing Florence's social skills.

Florence regarded ordinary life for a wealthy English woman as being useless and dull. Instead, she felt called to tend the sick and relieve what she saw as needless suffering. She often visited sick tenants on her family's estate, bringing them food and changing their bedding. Her family disapproved of this behavior as being unladylike. Next, she wanted to visit hospitals and learn about nursing. Her parents were horrified. Hospitals in Victorian England were terrible places. Wealthy people would never even think of going to a hospital; they were cared for at home. Hospitals were for the poor, who had no one else to care for them. Mr. and Mrs. Nightingale tried to distract young Florence by encouraging her to attend parties and to travel.

Florence was determined to serve the sick. She received encouragement to pursue her calling from Dr. Samuel Gridley Howe and his wife, Julia Ward Howe, the famous American abolitionists. Frances Nightingale was active in the antislavery movement and invited the Howes to the Nightingale estate in 1844. Dr. Howe assured Florence ". . . there is never anything unbecoming or unladylike in doing your duty for the good of others." That year, Florence began visiting hospitals, despite her parents' objections.

She found that English hospitals were filthy and crowded. The nurses were uneducated, untrained, and poorly paid. Often, they were drunk on the job and treated patients cruelly. Diseases spread rapidly in the dirty hospital wards, because no one knew that germs cause disease and infection. Any sick person who went to a hospital could expect to die rather than to get well. Back at home, Florence spent hours in her room thinking about the entire hospital system, why such conditions existed, and what could be done to improve them. She corresponded with people who could send her information about hospitals in other parts of the world. Eventually, she began to formulate ideas for hospital construction and administration that one day would be sought eagerly by many hospital planners.

During this time, Florence was being courted by one of England's most eligible bachelors. She was very fond of him and would have accepted his marriage proposal, but she feared that marriage would interfere with her calling to serve the poor and sickly. Finally, she had to reject him, which sent her into a deep depression.

To help raise her spirits, Florence's parents encouraged her to accompany friends on a tour of Europe and Egypt. She did so, but along the way she studied how the sick were cared for in other countries. She observed that patients who were clean and well-fed had a much better chance of recovery. She concluded that Roman Catholic nuns in France and women in Protestant nursing orders in Germany did a much better job of caring for the sick than nurses in England. She was particularly impressed with the German Institute of Deaconesses, a training school for nurses in the town of Kaiserswerth on the Rhine River near Düsseldorf. In 1851, she enrolled there for a four-month nursing course and then studied further at hospitals in Paris. In 1853, she was appointed superintendent of a women's hospital in London. She couldn't have been happier. At last she was able to start putting into practice her ideas on how to deliver better nursing care.

Then war broke out. In 1854, Britain, France, and their Turkish allies went to war with Russia in the Crimea. The British suffered heavy casualties, but hardly any provision had been made for care of the wounded. This situation was nothing new for the British army, which was plagued with bureaucracy and conflicting lines of command. However, the Crimean War was the first war to be covered by newspaper reporters, and stories about the callous way in which wounded British soldiers were treated soon caused a scandal in England. Without adequate supplies for their care, the wounded were left to die terrible deaths in rat-infested hospitals. The largest and worst of these was in Scutari, Turkey, across the Bosporus straits from what is now Istanbul. Wounded soldiers were shipped back to the hospital in Scutari by the hundreds in wagons and on boats. There, they were neglected, and many of them died needlessly.

By 1854, Nightingale already had developed a reputation for her nursing abilities. The secretary of war, who was a friend, asked if she would go to the battle area and try to improve hospital conditions. By coincidence, Nightingale had already sent him a letter volunteering her services. Immediately, she set about recruiting intelligent, able women for her nursing corps. Within a few days, she had signed up 38 and set out for Turkey and the barracks hospital at Scutari.

On arrival, she found a situation even worse than she had imagined. Thousands of soldiers, their wounds unattended, were lying in their own blood and excrement on filthy straw mattresses crawling with bugs. There were few real beds and no soap, blankets, or shirts for the men. The food was spoiled. At night, the medical officers went off to their quarters, leaving the wounded alone in the terrifying darkness of the hospital corridors. There weren't enough people to tend to the men.

Even so, the army officers were not pleased to see Nightingale and

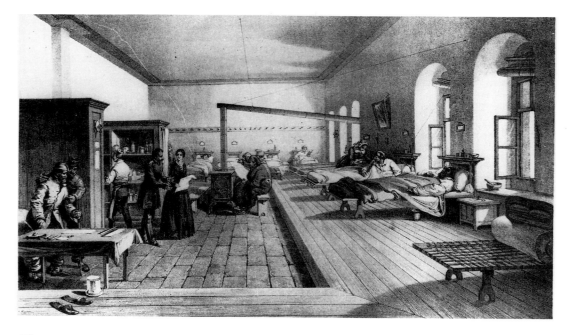

Florence Nightingale supervising a hospital during the Crimean War

her nurses. They resented being told how to care for the men; they were rude and uncooperative, insisting that an army hospital was no place for women. But Nightingale never had taken no for an answer. She had the support of the secretary of war and she also had good common sense in devising plans to win the support of the officers. Eventually, she and her nurses were able to set up diet kitchens and a laundry, scrub the floors, and see to it that the wounded men were clean and fed. The nurses also comforted the men by reading to them and talking with them. Nightingale made a habit of lighting a lantern at night and walking among the wounded soldiers to help dispel the terrors of the dark. Finally, she succeeded in having a sanitary team sent from England to Scutari to clean up the hospital, including the undrained cesspool on which it was built. As a result of her efforts to improve sanitary conditions, the death rate at Scutari dropped from 42 percent in February 1855 to 2 percent that June. The legend of the "lady with the lamp" began to grow.

The mere sight of Nightingale made the soldiers feel that all was well and that they would be cared for. They wrote letters home glorifying her nightly walks through the long, dark wards carrying her lamp and speaking softly to the soldiers. "What a comfort it was to see her pass," one wounded man wrote in a letter that became famous. "We lay there by the hundreds. But we could kiss her shadow as it fell and lay our heads on the pillow again, content."

The work Nightingale did in her quarters after working all day on the wards was equally important. She sent ingenious plans for reorganizing military hospitals back to the secretary of war. She urged him to keep military medical records and to establish an army medical school to train doctors in treating the types of sickness and wounds that occurred only on battlefields.

Nightingale visited the front lines in the Crimea to inspect the field hospitals. While there, she came down with an illness the doctors called Crimean fever. For almost two weeks, she was close to death. All of England, from Queen Victoria to common foot soldiers, prayed for her recovery. Recover she did, but her health was severely damaged. She remained a semi-invalid for the rest of her life.

In 1856, the war ended, and Nightingale returned to England. She was a celebrity, but she preferred to live privately and quietly, first at her family home and later in London. Nevertheless, she had many famous and influential friends, including Elizabeth Blackwell, the first modern woman doctor.

Florence Nightingale's work was far from done. She wrote reports and completed studies on health and sanitation problems in various places throughout the British Empire, including India. In 1860, she used money collected by the public to found the Nightingale Training School for Nurses at St. Thomas's Hospital in London.

She was regarded by the entire world as the foremost authority on nursing, which she had raised to a respectable profession. She insisted that nurses should not do cleaning and scrubbing. "A nurse should do nothing but nurse," she wrote. "If you want a charwoman, have one. Nursing is a specialty." She called for the use of efficient systems and devices, such as having hot water piped into patients' rooms and dumb-waiters to lift food from the kitchens to the nursing floors. She also advocated a system whereby bedridden patients could call for a nurse with the use of specially designed bells.

For the rest of her life, Nightingale was called upon by governments all over the world to advise on matters of nursing and sanitation. Despite her frail health, she lived to the age of ninety, and died in her London home on August 13, 1910.

Clara Barton

Founder of the American Red Cross

1821–1912

Even as a young girl, Clara Barton was very practical. Instead of playing with toys, she learned how to do things—from hammering nails to sewing dresses. When a need arose, she was quick to find a practical way to fill it. These qualities were to bring her lasting fame. During the American Civil War, she saw wounded Union soldiers in need of food, blankets, and medical supplies, and she moved quickly to fill that need by asking volunteers to donate goods and services to aid the troops. She then saw the need for organized aid to help those suffering not only from war but also from natural disasters. She devoted much of her life to filling this need, by founding and directing a nationwide disaster relief organization—the American National Red Cross.

Clara Barton was born on Christmas Day, 1821, in the town of North Oxford, Massachusetts. She was the fifth child of Stephen and Sarah Barton, who named her Clarissa. She preferred to be called Clara. Clara's brothers and sisters were all at least ten years older, so there was no one at home to play with. Rather than play, she spent her time learning from her entire family.

Her father, who had fought under the command of General Anthony Wayne when the army defeated an uprising of Indian tribes in Ohio, was fond of telling stories about his army days to Clara. And her brothers were always willing to teach her how to build and fix things. From her mother and sisters, she learned to cook and do household tasks. Clara also attended a boarding school in a nearby town.

Because of an unfortunate accident when she was eleven, she gained practical experience in nursing. Her brother David was helping tear down a barn when a wall fell on him. Clara was given the job of caring for him as he recovered from his injury.

Clara's family may have thought of her as something of a problem child. She was painfully shy and timid and was overly sensitive to criticism. In an autobiographical account of her childhood, she wrote, "I remember nothing but fear." Yet, she was wilful, always wanting to do things her own way. An acquaintance of the family sensed that what Clara needed was a challenge. "Throw responsibility upon her," he advised. "As soon as her age will permit, give her a school to teach." And so, at the age of fifteen, Clara Barton began her professional life as a teacher.

She was very good at her work, and after taking more training at a school in Clinton, New York, she was offered a teaching position at a private school in Bordentown, New Jersey. There she first displayed her extraordinary skill at seeing a need and how to fill it.

In the 1850s, most schools in the United States were private. Children whose parents could not afford to pay simply did not go to school. Barton saw these children in Bordentown and concluded that they needed an education. She persuaded the townspeople to set up a free school; she even offered to teach there without pay. She began with six pupils, but soon the school grew to include some six hundred. To accommodate this success, the town needed a new building and more teachers. But the very success of Barton's school disturbed the town leaders. No woman, they decided, could administer such a sizable operation. In 1854, they hired a man to supervise her. Incensed, she resigned.

She moved to Washington, D.C., and with the help of a family friend obtained a job as a clerk in the U.S. Patent Office. In 1854, women were an unusual sight in any office. Barton had to put up with insults and harassment from her male co-workers. Her supervisors appreciated the fine quality of her work, but somehow she felt useless. Something was missing in her life.

All that changed in 1861, when war broke out between the states. After the first battle of Bull Run in July, Barton watched thousands of defeated Union soldiers retreating to Washington. There were not enough bandages or medical supplies for the wounded, and there were few other items to comfort the disheartened troops, many of whom were young men away from home for the first time in their lives. Barton swung into action. First, she tore up her own sheets to make bandages. Then, she put a notice in a Massachusetts newspaper calling for donations of food, medicine, and bandages. The donations came pouring in, and Barton and some friends set about distributing them to the soldiers.

Next, she insisted upon bringing these supplies right to the battlefield, where they were needed most. She overcame the resistance of army officers and surgeons, acquired a wagon and team of mules, and rode out to the sites of many major battles, including the second battle of Bull Run, Antietam, and Fredericksburg. When the cannons roared and the bullets flew, Barton and her volunteers would be there, making gallons of soup and coffee and baking thousands of loaves of bread. In one famous episode, Barton was holding a fallen soldier so that he might take a drink, when a bullet flew under her arm and killed the man. The bullet tore the sleeve of her dress. She never mended it. The soldiers who saw this short, brown-haired woman coming to aid them, one hand lifting the hem of her skirt out of the mud and blood, took to calling her the "Angel of the Battlefield."

After the war ended in 1865, Barton undertook the task of trying to identify those missing in action. In the Civil War cemeteries, there were more than 315,000 graves—but less than 173,000 carried name markers. She posted ads in newspapers and set up an office to gather information from returned soldiers about those known to have been killed. Whatever she learned, she passed on to the grieving families. At Andersonville, a notorious Confederate camp for prisoners of war in Georgia, Barton was able to identify and mark the graves of almost thirteen thousand men.

A lecture tour followed her Civil War work and both took a toll on Barton's health. In 1869, she set off on a tour of Europe, seeking rest and relaxation. Instead she found a cause that would occupy her for the rest of her life and save the lives of countless others in the future.

While visiting Switzerland, she learned of a recently formed organization called the International Committee of the Red Cross. The Red Cross had been founded in 1863 by Jean Henri Dunant, a Swiss man, who, like Barton, had been horrified by the suffering of soldiers wounded in war. In 1864, diplomats from twelve European nations met in Geneva, Switzerland, to draft the Geneva Convention, a document that called for nations to organize groups like the Red Cross that would help relieve the suffering of soldiers captured or wounded.

In 1870, war broke out between France and Prussia, a German state. Eventually, all of Germany became involved. Barton served with the International Red Cross during this Franco-Prussian conflict and became convinced that the United States should ratify the Geneva Convention and form a Red Cross organization. Not everyone agreed. The United States feared getting too involved with foreign powers, and many American leaders saw this as just such an entanglement.

When Barton returned home in 1873, she took on the task of convincing the U.S. president and Senate to ratify the Geneva Convention. She had a vision of a national Red Cross headquarters with state and local chapters branching off from it. The American Red Cross would aid war victims and send doctors, nurses, and relief workers to help victims of floods, fires, and earthquakes. For eight years, she lobbied lawmakers, lectured, and wrote articles. Finally, on March 1, 1882, President Chester A. Arthur signed the treaty, and the Senate later ratified it.

Barton became the first president of the American Association of the Red Cross, which she and her supporters had founded in 1881. In 1893, the organization was chartered as the American National Red Cross. She remained its president until 1904, and during that time she and her trusted aide, Dr. Julian B. Hubbell, personally supervised relief efforts at such emergencies as the Johnstown, Pennsylvania, flood; floods of the Ohio and Mississippi rivers; a yellow-fever epidemic in Florida; and a hurricane that struck the Georgia coast. At the age of seventy-seven, she went to the aid of soldiers in the Spanish-American war with her mules and wagons as she had during the Civil War.

Barton controlled all aspects of the Red Cross, from deciding which situations called for Red Cross relief to handling the organization's finances. She refused all government funding, but times were changing and the organization was growing beyond the limits of what one individual could do. In the early 1900s, controversy over its administration broke out, and Barton resigned. She continued to write and lecture, and in 1906 founded the National First-Aid Association of America.

On April 12, 1912, at the age of ninety-one, Barton passed away at her thirty-eight-room home in Glen Echo, Maryland, which for a number of years had served as headquarters for the American Red Cross. Her remains were buried in North Oxford, Massachusetts. In 1974, the Glen Echo home was named the Clara Barton National Historic Site.

Today, the organization Clara Barton founded provides many basic medical services. It collects and distributes about 50 percent of the donated blood in the United States and operates a national transplant service, providing bone, skin, and organs. The Red Cross also offers courses in first aid, cardiopulmonary resuscitation, accident prevention, and basic health education.

Systems and Schools of Medicine

———————◆———————

T he first doctors to write down specific instructions for treating different types of illness and injuries came from the earliest civilizations in Egypt and Mesopotamia. Because the cause of illness was a great mystery, these early medical systems relied heavily on religion and magic for cures. Along with prayers and chants, the early physicians recorded surgical treatments for injuries, boils, and skin cancers. Rarely, however, did any primitive surgeon dare to cut very deeply into the body. Nevertheless, one of the earliest surgical operations was trephining, cutting out small pieces of the skull. Anthropologists have seen evidence of trephining in skulls found all over the world. They think that prehistoric people used trephining to release spirits believed to cause headaches, mental disorders, or epilepsy.

The first people to look for natural, rather than supernatural, causes of disease were the ancient Greeks. The most renowned of these Greek physicians was Hippocrates, credited with writing many medical texts and with calling upon physicians to uphold high moral and ethical standards. Hippocrates believed that illness resulted from imbalances in substances called humors. In his view, the most important role of a physician was to prevent illness by keeping the humors in balance. The way to do this was by bleeding— opening a vein in the patient's arm and removing blood—or by purging—giving doses of powerful laxatives or drugs that cause vomiting.

Although the Hippocratic system was the most influential in Greek medicine, alternative systems sprang up. One system held that illness resulted from disordered atoms in the body and could be cured by exercise, massage, and baths. Another blamed improper breathing for illnesses. Yet another school of medical thought, called "eclectic," advocated picking and choosing from among the best of Hippocratic and alternative treatments.

Into this situation came Galen, a physician born in Greece and made famous in Rome. He lived between A.D. 129 and 199, but he influenced medicine and treatment until the 1800s. His thinking was brilliant—even though we now know that much of it was wrong. He came from the eclectic tradition, but developed a system of medicine based mainly on the teaching of Hippocrates. He explained the workings of the human body in a complex but very rational way that combined the balance of four humors—substances that he thought circulated in the blood—with breathing, environmental factors, diet, and digestion. He believed it was better to prevent illness than to try and cure it. When treatment was necessary, he prescribed bleeding, purging, and diuretics, substances that increase the flow of urine.

There were no major discoveries in medicine in Europe during the early Middle Ages, but Arab physicians continued to make progress from the ninth through the eleventh centuries, describing measles, meningitis, tetanus, and smallpox. An Arab physician, Avicenna, wrote the *Canon of Medicine,* a medical encyclopedia that summed up all the medical knowledge of the time. Christian crusaders to the Holy Land brought Avicenna's work back to Europe, where it influenced medicine for the next 600 years.

The first major challenge to the humoral theory of medicine came from a Swiss alchemist and physician named Paracelsus, who lived from about 1493 to 1541. He believed that each illness had a specific cause outside the body. He also was the first to try treating illness with chemicals, such as arsenic, iron, mercury, and sulphur.

At the same time, Flemish physician Andreas Vesalius (1514-1564) began making careful dissections of dead bodies—a practice forbidden by the church—and made important contributions to the knowledge of human anatomy with his book *On the Structure of the Human Body*. The Renaissance and the establishment of scientific medicine was underway. In 1628, English physician William Harvey published a book documenting his discovery of the circulation of the blood and the action of the heart as a pump. During the 1700s and 1800s, instruments were invented to measure body temperature, see microscopic organisms, and listen to heartbeats.

There were few improvements, however, in the actual treatments for disease. The regular medical system, called allopathy, offered "heroic" treatments to restore balance to the humors in the body. These treatments were truly horrible and no doubt caused many deaths. In fact, repeated bleedings may have contributed to the death of George Washington after he fell ill with what was probably strep throat.

In addition to razors for opening veins, the regular doctor's bag included leeches for drawing blood from specific areas of the body; emetics to cause vomiting; enemas and laxatives; devices for causing blisters on the skin; patches to plaster on various body parts; and powerful addictive drugs based on opium for relieving pain and nervous tension.

In reaction to these terrible treatments, alternative, or irregular, systems of medicine came into being. One of the most popular was homeopathy, developed by German physician Samuel Hahnemann in the late 1700s. This system was based on the notion that "like cures like;" that is, the way to treat an illness is with a substance that produces the same effect as the disease. A homeopathic treatment for an itchy rash, for example, might be made from a plant that causes an itchy rash. Homeopathic remedies often contain poisons, but they are diluted so much that almost nothing of the poison remains. Hahnemann believed that the more diluted a drug was the more powerful it became.

Other systems included hydropathy (water cures), osteopathy (a holistic system), and chiropractic (based on proper alignment of bones and muscles). The eclectic system drew what seemed to be the best treatments from all the competing systems. The followers of each medical system established their own medical schools. The irregular schools were the first to admit women.

In the mid-1800s, great discoveries were made that revolutionized regular, allopathic medicine. Anesthesia allowed doctors to perform ever more complex operations. The knowledge that germs cause disease led to sterile surgical techniques that greatly reduced deadly infections. Specific germs were identified as the causes of specific diseases. By the 1940s, antibiotics and other drugs had been developed to treat bacterial infections. Vaccines wiped out one infectious threat after another. Miraculous operations were developed to cure heart ailments, to transplant organs, and to treat diseases of the brain. By the 1990s, a new revolution, based on genetics, was occurring in medicine. Genes responsible for hereditary illnesses were being identified, and effective treatments for genetic diseases were within the realm of possibility. Damage to genetic material was identified as the underlying cause of some diseases, including cancer.

Even though regular medicine became more successful at treating specific ills, patients became more dissatisfied with regular medicine. In the 1990s, large numbers of people were once again turning to alternative medicine. Social commentators offered a variety of explanations. Perhaps people's expectations of medical miracles were just too high; if an illness could not be cured easily by conventional medicine, they turned to the promise of alternatives. Some people did not like what they regarded as highly invasive treatments—such as inserting balloons through arteries to clear them of blockages.

Other critics believed that medical practice had become too specialized. Many doctors were treating only the illness without regard to the entire person. As a result, a trend toward "holistic" medicine developed. Many medical doctors now believe that it is important to consider every aspect of a person's life in order to treat effectively—but more importantly to prevent—the development of disease.

Elizabeth Blackwell

First Woman Doctor of Modern Times

1821–1910

Wrenching change and emotional hardship were no strangers to Elizabeth Blackwell. At age eleven, she had to leave her home in England when her family moved to America. At seventeen, her beloved father died, and she and her mother and sisters had to find a way to support the financially strapped household. As an adult, she decided to pursue a career in medicine, and had to endure ignorance, prejudice, taunts, and insults. But this determined woman of vision went on to become the first woman to receive a degree from a medical school in the United States, becoming the first woman doctor of modern times.

Elizabeth Blackwell was born near Bristol, England, on February 3, 1821, into the well-to-do family of Hannah and Samuel Blackwell, who owned a sugar refinery. The Blackwells were a most unusual family. Samuel and Hannah believed strongly in civil liberties and supported social reforms, including the abolition of slavery. They believed that girls, as well as boys, should have a good education. However, the best schools were controlled by the Church of England and were open only to church members. The Blackwell family did not belong to the church, so Elizabeth and her sisters and brothers were educated at home by private tutors.

The Blackwell household was a lively one. It grew to nine surviving children, the parents, and Samuel's four unmarried sisters. Books and music played a central role in family life, and all the children loved to dance.

In 1832, life for the Blackwells changed radically. The sugar refinery burned down, and Samuel decided there were better opportunities for him in America. So the family sailed off to find a new home in New York City. Samuel soon became deeply involved in the abolitionist movement. As a result, Elizabeth and the other Blackwell children came to know major leaders of the antislavery movement, who often visited in their home to discuss this great moral issue. The Blackwells also were supporters of the new movement to win voting rights for women. Two of the Blackwell boys married leaders of the women's rights movement.

In America, Samuel opened another sugar refinery. To avoid using sugar cane, which was harvested by slave labor, he experimented with refining sugar from beets. He was not very successful, however, and during a financial depression in 1837, Samuel suffered big losses.

Convinced that he could do better farther west, Samuel moved the family to Cincinnati, Ohio, in May 1838. But disaster struck again. Samuel died in August, leaving the Blackwell family destitute.

To survive, Elizabeth, her mother, and sisters opened a boarding school, at which Elizabeth taught for four years. It seemed at first that her career would be that of a teacher. Becoming a doctor was the farthest thing from her mind. She always had been repelled by anything connected with the human body and admitted that physical ailments filled her with disgust. For a year, she headed a girls' school in Kentucky, but the local pro-slavery attitudes were too much for her social conscience, so she returned to Cincinnati.

The idea of becoming a doctor grew out of a conversation with a woman friend who was dying of cancer and who believed strongly that women physicians could provide better care for women patients. She urged Elizabeth to take up medicine. At first, the idea was not appealing to Elizabeth, but the more she thought about it, the better it seemed. Women were accepted as midwives and nurses, but no woman ever had been admitted to a medical school. At that time women had almost no rights and were not welcome in institutions of higher learning. Elizabeth, however, believed in education for women. "The idea of winning a doctor's degree gradually assumed the aspect of a great moral struggle," Dr. Blackwell later wrote in her autobiography, "and the moral fight possessed immense attraction for me."

To earn money for her medical education, she continued to teach at schools in North and South Carolina for two more years. She also studied medicine privately with male physicians who were sympathetic to her cause. In 1847, she began to apply to medical schools, beginning with the best available. She was turned down by Harvard and by every major school to which she applied in Philadelphia and New York City. One sympathetic male doctor suggested she disguise herself as a man in order to get accepted. Undeterred, she applied to less reputable medical colleges in rural areas.

Finally, Elizabeth was accepted by the Geneva Medical College in western New York State. However, her acceptance came about because the students thought that having a woman in their class would be a hilarious prank. The school administrators, not knowing what to do with her application, had put it to a vote by the all-male student body. The students lightheartedly and unanimously voted "yes."

When a petite blond woman showed up for class, the students realized it was far from a joke. The people in the town where the school was located thought that a woman who wanted to be a doctor must be very odd and, in all likelihood, immoral. They shunned her, but most of the students came to accept Blackwell. Her intelligence, dignity, and iron-willed determination eventually won the admiration of teachers and students alike. In 1849, Elizabeth Blackwell graduated as the first woman doctor of medicine.

Her next goal was to become a surgeon. Medical education in the United States was not very good, even at the best schools. So Blackwell decided to study in Europe, where great medical advances were starting to occur. She went first to England, where she was greeted as something of a celebrity and welcomed by many doctors. But she wanted to study where the best schools were—in France.

France, at the time, was the leader in a concept called clinical medicine. The French physicians believed that diseases could be described and diagnosed by carefully observing patients and their symptoms. Before, doctors usually just asked patients questions, then came up with a vague diagnosis based on an imbalance in substances they called "humors." The French clinicians, to make ever better observations, invented many new instruments, including the stethoscope for listening to heartbeats.

However, the French were not enthusiastic about a woman doctor. They said she only was welcome to attend their internationally renowned school for midwives, along with all the young girls from the countryside and city. Dr. Blackwell accepted this offer, because she saw it as an opportunity to study obstetrics and gynecology at one of the greatest institutions in the world.

A tragic accident there ended Elizabeth's dreams of becoming a surgeon. While washing out the infected eye of an infant, Dr. Blackwell's left eye was spattered with contaminated fluid. As a result, her eye became so infected that she eventually lost sight in it. It was a wrenching physical and emotional ordeal. When she was well enough, she returned to England to recuperate. Again, she was greeted as a celebrity, and she counted among her many admirers Florence Nightingale, who went on to establish the profession of nursing and became a lifelong friend of Dr. Blackwell.

When Elizabeth Blackwell returned to New York City in 1851, she was received very differently. No clinic or hospital would hire her as a physician. Dr. Blackwell even had trouble renting space for her private practice, and she had very few patients. She turned her attention to lecturing and writing about the importance of good hygiene. Dr. Blackwell was a strong believer in preventive medicine and felt that good nutrition and proper sanitation played key roles. In this belief she was ahead of her time.

Those early years in New York City were very lonely ones for her. So she went to an orphanage for children of immigrants and adopted a seven-year-old Irish orphan, Kitty Barry, who stayed with Dr. Blackwell all her life.

One day, a group of Quaker women attended Dr. Blackwell's lectures and were so impressed that they became her patients and recommended her to their friends. Dr. Blackwell's practice began to grow, but she also wanted to do something to relieve the suffering of immigrants in New York's overcrowded tenement slums. In 1853, Dr. Blackwell established a one-room clinic to serve poor women. In the first year, she

The New York Infirmary for Women and Children, which was established by Elizabeth Blackwell

treated some two hundred women. Soon, she was joined by her sister, Emily, who also had become a physician, and by another young woman doctor, Marie Zakrzewska. Within a few years, the one-room clinic had expanded to become the New York Infirmary for Women and Children, which formally opened in 1857.

In the summer of 1858, Elizabeth Blackwell left Emily in charge of the hospital and went back to England for a year to help further the cause of medical education for women. In January 1859, hers became the first woman's name entered in the British medical register, giving her the right to practice medicine in England. After that, the British medical establishment made sure that no other woman's name would be allowed on the register. It was many years before women doctors were accepted in Britain.

After returning to New York, Dr. Blackwell spent the next several years making plans to establish a medical school for women. Her plans had to be postponed when the Civil War broke out. Both Elizabeth and Emily Blackwell set to work, helping recruit and train nurses to care for wounded soldiers.

In 1868, Elizebeth Blackwell's plans became reality: the Woman's Medical College of the New York Infirmary finally opened. She made sure that the school would have the highest standards. Medical education at that time was anything but standardized, and many of the colleges—even for men—offered only a few months of extremely poor medical education. The only scientific course taught was anatomy. But Dr. Blackwell established entrance examinations for her school, set up a three-year course of study, made sure the students had plenty of practical clinical experience, and created an independent examining board of the best-known physicians in New York City.

Having accomplished this, Elizabeth left the operation of the school to Emily and returned to England—this time for good. Even though she was a naturalized United States citizen, she lived the rest of her life in England. She was more interested in studying the moral and social aspects of medicine than the practical and scientific ones. But she developed a private practice in London and in 1875 became chair of gynecology at the London School of Medicine for Women, newly founded by the pioneering Sophia Jex-Blake. Although she lectured only for one year because of poor health, Dr. Blackwell held this post until 1907. That year, she fell down a flight of stairs at her summer residence in Scotland. She never fully recovered and died on May 31, 1910.

Lydia Folger Fowler

First American Woman Doctor

1822–1879

The first women's rights convention, held in 1848 at Seneca Falls, New York, drew fire from male journalists, politicians, and preachers. The radical women and their male friends had dared to issue a Declaration of Sentiments, demanding better educational and job opportunities for women, as well as the right to vote. Surprisingly, at least one group of men—medical men—thought this was a good idea. They set about organizing a medical school at which men and women would be equally welcome, the first of its kind in America. When the Central Medical College of New York opened its doors in Syracuse in 1849, Lydia Folger Fowler was among the first to enroll. She also was the first woman to graduate from this school, and thus became the first American woman doctor.

Lydia Folger was born on May 5, 1822, on the whaling island of Nantucket, Massachusetts. She was one of seven children born to Gideon and Eunice Folger. The Folger family was very prominent in early American history. Benjamin Franklin was a distant Folger relative, as were the pioneering woman astronomer, Maria Mitchell, and the abolitionist and women's rights advocate, Lucretia Mott. In fact, Maria Mitchell's father was one of Lydia Folger's teachers. He introduced both Maria and Lydia to the universe of the stars by taking them to rooftops where they could view the wonderful nighttime sky. With such a family as this, young Lydia was encouraged to learn all she could. Outside Nantucket and the family circle, the world of learning was not a very friendly place for women. They were not welcome at colleges or universities and certainly not at medical schools.

In 1844 after teaching for two years at Wheaton Seminary in Norton, Massachusetts, Lydia Folger married Lorenzo Niles Fowler, one of the world's most renowned phrenologists. Phrenology was one of many pseudosciences (false sciences) sweeping the world in the mid-1800s. Phrenologists believed that character, talents, and personality were controlled by different areas of the brain, which they called organs. Furthermore, the phrenologists claimed, there are bumps and bulges on the skull above these various organs. A "map" made by feeling a person's skull for the biggest bulges could tell a great deal about the individual. Certain patterns of bumps would indicate talents for particular fields, such as literature, art, or mathematics. Other bumps indicated honesty, kind-heartedness, or even criminal tendencies.

Phrenology was actually an early attempt at brain mapping. There were no sophisticated brain scanners available then, so the people doing these investigations made the best guess they could at what was responsible for mind-body links.

Lydia Folger Fowler became very interested in phrenology, as well as in anatomy, physiology, and hygiene. She wrote books on these topics, which were published by the family publishing company of Fowlers & Wells, and she lectured to women's groups. Her message would be familiar today: Get plenty of fresh air and exercise, avoid rich foods, don't smoke or drink alcohol, and avoid coffee and tea. What was most radical for her time was advice to bathe every day. People in the mid-1800s still believed that bathing might be bad for the health and that a bath every month or so was enough.

Obviously, Lydia Fowler had a great talent for and interest in the medical arts. When the Central Medical College opened in 1849, she not only was among the first to enroll, she was the best prepared because of her independent studies. Although there were several women in her class, she graduated before them in June 1850, becoming the first American-born woman doctor and the second woman to receive a medical degree in the United States. (The first was Elizabeth Blackwell, a British immigrant, who received her M.D. degree in 1849.) In 1851, the school, by then called Rochester Eclectic Medical College, appointed Dr. Fowler professor of midwifery and diseases of women and children, making her the first woman professor at an American medical school. Her career as professor was brief, however, because the school closed in 1852.

Rochester Eclectic Medical College, like most American medical schools, did not have very high standards. It was called a sectarian school. Various medical schools of thought, or sects, in the mid- to late 1800s were putting forth alternative theories to those held by the regular, mainstream medical profession. This was not surprising, considering the terrible treatments and totally incorrect theory of disease held by the regular doctors, who believed that mysterious substances called humors were responsible for disease. The cure for almost anything was to get rid of bad humors by giving the patient powerful laxatives and drugs to cause vomiting, or by opening a vein and drawing out large quantities of blood. Often the treatment was far worse than the illness, and the patient died from dehydration or loss of blood.

The competing sectarian theories were no more scientific and the treatments no more effective, but they were gentler. One of the sects was homeopathy. Another sect believed in water cures, consisting largely of bathing and drinking large quantities of water. Eclectic physicians tried to take the best from all the various sects and use them in medical practice.

The early women physicians, such as Dr. Fowler, concluded it was better to concentrate on health education and disease prevention than to try to cure people with the treatments available. From 1852 to 1860, she lectured to women about preventive health care while maintaining a private practice in New York City. She also campaigned for more women doctors. She believed that many women in need of medical care were too modest to seek the advice of a male physician.

In 1860, she went to Europe with her husband, who was on a lecture tour, and studied medicine in England and France. In 1861, she returned to the United States and lectured for a year on midwifery at a sectarian medical school in New York City. The Fowlers then sailed again for London, where they remained for the rest of their lives. Lydia Fowler gave up the practice of medicine and became very active in the temperance movement. Dr. Fowler died of pneumonia in London on January 26, 1879, at the age of fifty-six.

Emily Blackwell

Physician and Surgeon

1826–1910

When Emily Blackwell decided to become a doctor, she had an inspiring role model to follow. Her sister, Elizabeth, was the first woman to receive a recognized medical degree in the United States and the first woman doctor of modern times. The Blackwell sisters were a strong team to open the medical profession to women. While Elizabeth was a visionary and dreamer, Emily was a practical person and became one of the best physicians and surgeons of that time. Together they founded a hospital for women and children, but it was Emily who took it over and guided the New York Infirmary to great success.

Emily Blackwell was born into the family of a well-to-do sugar refiner near Bristol, England, on October 8, 1826. But after her father's refinery burned, the family moved to the United States. Emily was only five years old when the family took up residence in New York; they later moved to New Jersey and then to Ohio.

The Blackwells were a liberal family, devoted to the cause of abolishing slavery. Emily's father and mother invited many of the greatest names in the abolitionist movement to their home. As a result, Emily counted among her friends such progressive thinkers as Henry Ward Beecher and Harriet Beecher Stowe.

Emily and her eight brothers and sisters were given equal educations by private tutors, because her parents believed that women should have the same opportunities as men. This was a radical idea for the mid-1800s, when most young ladies were taught only how to run a household, play the piano, and be a charming companion for men. Emily knew how to play the piano and played very well. But she also loved to do scientific experiments in the attic of the Blackwell home and to go outdoors to observe nature. She developed an extensive knowledge of flowers and birds.

After Elizabeth made the pioneering journey into medicine, Emily decided to follow. But there were some significant differences between the two sisters, their temperaments, and their motivations. Elizabeth was small, blond, and very self-confident. She also had no natural interest in medicine. Instead, she saw her effort to become a doctor as a great moral issue involving equal rights for women. Emily was tall, redheaded, and extremely shy. She had a great interest in scientific subjects. When Emily told Elizabeth of her decision to study medicine, Elizabeth gave her every encouragement. She also warned Emily that being a woman doctor was a painfully lonely life filled with "social and professional antagonism."

From the beginning, Emily experienced this antagonism. First, she had difficulty getting into a respectable medical school. The Geneva Medical College that had graduated Elizabeth decided not to make the mistake of admitting a woman again. They rejected Emily's application, as did nine other medical schools. In the summer of 1852, Rush Medical College in Chicago took Emily as a student. But the State Medical Society criticized Rush for accepting a woman, and after one year of study she had to leave. By now, Dr. Elizabeth Blackwell had set up a clinic for poor women in New York City, and Emily spent the summer working there. Finally, she was admitted to what is now the medical school of Case Western Reserve University in Cleveland. She graduated with honors in 1854.

Like all new graduates who wanted to become good doctors, Emily went abroad for further study. All the major advances in medicine were being made in Britain, France, and Germany. Dr. Emily Blackwell chose first to study with Sir James Young Simpson in Edinburgh, Scotland. Simpson was rocking the medical world with the radical idea of painless childbirth. He used chloroform to put the birthing mother to sleep.

Emily Blackwell then went to the Children's Hospital in London, where she worked and studied with Dr. William Jenner, who was making great advances in the diagnosis and treatment of typhoid and other communicable diseases. She also studied new surgical techniques and observed medical treatment in the clinics of Paris, Berlin, and Dresden. Two years later, she returned to America, a skilled surgeon and one of the best-educated doctors in the world.

She immediately joined her sister and another pioneering woman doctor, Marie Zakrzewska, in the task of creating a hospital for poor women and children. Unlike Elizabeth and Dr. Zakrzewska, Emily never went into private practice. She devoted her career to the New York Infirmary for Women and Children, which opened in 1857. Dr. Emily Blackwell was in charge of surgery, but she also helped out with nursing, housekeeping, and fund-raising events.

The hospital began to expand in size and scope. A nursing school was added in 1858, and the infirmary had to move to a larger building in 1860. Emily was able to get state funding, and in 1866 added a Tenement House Service, employing workers who went into the tenements, giving out practical information on hygiene, as well as providing nursing care for the poor.

In 1868, Dr. Elizabeth Blackwell founded a women's medical school in association with the hospital, and the next year moved to England, leaving Dr. Emily Blackwell in charge of both the hospital and the school. Under Emily's care, the hospital and the medical college continued to expand and grow. By 1893, the medical college had almost ninety students enrolled in its four-year course of study. Few medical schools in America had such rigorous requirements or offered such high-quality education. Many students who would become famous doctors passed though its doors, including Dr. S. Josephine Baker and cancer research pioneer Dr. Elise L'Esperance. They all acknowledged the debt they owed to Dr. Emily. "She inspired us all with the vital feeling that we were still on trial and that, for women who meant to be physicians, no educational standards could be too high," wrote Dr. Baker. "I think not many of us realized that we were going out into the world as test cases, but Dr. Blackwell did."

In 1898, Cornell University Medical College decided to accept women. The following year, Dr. Emily, who believed in coeducation, took this opportunity to merge her medical college with that of Cornell. By then, 364 women doctors had graduated from the Women's Medical College.

In 1900, Dr. Emily Blackwell retired, spending summers on the coast of Maine and winters in Montclair, New Jersey, and visiting with Anna, her adopted daughter. She died on September 7, 1910, in her home at York Cliffs, Maine, just three months after the death of her sister, Elizabeth.

Sarah P. Remond

African–American
Physician and
Activist

1826-1894

A Mozart opera was to be performed at the Howard Athenaeum in May 1853, and Sarah Remond and two friends decided they would enjoy seeing it. When they arrived at the theater, they were told they would have to sit in a section segregated from the white operagoers. Furious, they refused. The theater management called the police to forcibly remove Sarah and her friends. The policemen grabbed Sarah roughly, and she fell down a flight of stairs. She went to court over the incident and won not only a five-hundred-dollar settlement but a moral victory for the cause of equal rights.

Sarah Remond was one of the first African-American women physicians. But she became far more famous for her work in the antislavery and women's rights movements.

Sarah Parker Remond was born on June 6, 1826, in Salem, Massachusetts, one of six girls and two boys in the Remond family. Her mother, Nancy, was a baker and the daughter of an American Revolutionary War veteran. Sarah's father, John, immigrated to Massachusetts from the Caribbean island of Curaçao in 1798 and became a well-known hairdresser and wig maker. Ornamental wigs were all the rage in fashions of the 1700s and early 1800s.

The Remond household was a haven for abolitionists and reformers. Sarah grew up listening to the conversations and speeches of leaders such as William Lloyd Garrison and Frederick Douglass. Sarah's brother, Charles, became a prominent antislavery lecturer.

Despite the Remond family's prominent position, Sarah and other black children faced discrimination in the Salem public schools. In 1834, the school committee decided to set up a separate school for African-American children. In 1835, when Sarah was ready for high school, she was not allowed to enroll. Nancy and John Remond were not about to stand for such discrimination. They moved the family to Newport, Rhode Island, and enrolled the children at a private school there. In 1841, they all returned to Salem, and Sarah continued to educate herself by reading books and newspapers. She also was active in local antislavery organizations and went with her brother, Charles, on public-speaking engagements.

In 1856, she was hired as a lecturer by the American Anti-Slavery Society. She shared the platform with such great activists as Susan B. Anthony and Wendell Phillips. In 1859, she went on a lecture tour of England, Ireland, and Scotland. She drew huge crowds, who listened to her eloquent speeches detailing the horrors of slavery and providing powerful arguments for why the practice must be ended.

Despite these successes, Sarah never felt that she had the opportunity for the type of education she really wanted. She wrote a friend: ". . . Although my heart was in the work [of lecturing], I felt that I was in need of a good English education. . . . And when I consider that the only reason why I did not obtain what I so much desired was because I was the possessor of an unpopular complexion, it adds to my discomfort." In 1859, she enrolled at the Bedford College for Ladies in London, and studied math, history, geography, literature, French, Latin, and music there until 1861.

During this time, she also continued to travel and lecture. In one highly publicized incident, the American legation (diplomatic mission) in London refused her a visa to visit France on the grounds that she was a person of color and such persons did not have the rights of United States citizenship. She got to France anyway. Then, during the Civil War, she helped pressure the British to honor the Union blockade of Confederate harbors.

When the Civil War ended, she returned to the United States for a brief time and took up the cause of women's rights. However, she felt more comfortable in the less prejudiced atmosphere of Europe, and soon returned to England. In 1866, she moved to Florence, Italy, where she enrolled as a medical student at the Santa Maria Nuova Hospital. She completed her training in 1868. Although there are no official records of her graduation, she apparently was certified to practice medicine. A friend who visited her in 1873 wrote that she was "winning a fine position in Florence as a physician."

Little more is known of Sarah Remond's life. In 1877, she married an Italian named Lazzaro Pinto. At some point, she apparently moved to Rome, because a letter from Frederick Douglass mentions visiting the Remonds there. By this time two of Sarah's sisters had joined her. She died on December 13, 1894, at the age of sixty-eight, and was buried in the Protestant cemetery in Rome.

The First African-American Women Doctors

In the mid-1800s, it was difficult for a white woman to become a doctor. It was doubly difficult for a black woman to pursue this profession. Nevertheless, several African-American women beat the odds and earned M.D.s.

Who was the first African-American woman to become a doctor? The historical record is not entirely clear, but it probably was a woman named Rebecca Lee. She graduated from the New England Female Medical College in Boston in 1864—just before the Civil War—and practiced medicine in Richmond, Virginia. But not many details are known about her life.

More is known about Rebecca J. Cole, the first black woman to graduate from the Women's Medical College of Pennsylvania. She was born on March 16, 1848, in Philadelphia, one of five children. The Cole children all received good educations. Rebecca graduated from the Institute for Colored Youth in Philadelphia, a school that had been founded by a Quaker to educate black boys and girls. She taught briefly before enrolling in the Female (Woman's) Medical College of Pennsylvania, from which she graduated in 1867.

She then went to New York City and served as resident physician at the New York Infirmary for Women and Children, a hospital established by Elizabeth Blackwell, the first woman doctor of modern times. While at the New York Infirmary, Dr. Cole served the needs of poor women in slum areas of the city by educating them on how to care for their babies and the health of their families. After holding posts in North Carolina and Washington, D.C., she returned to Philadelphia and set up a private practice. Along with another physician, Charlotte Abby, she founded a service called the Medical Directory that gave both medical and legal aid to women. Dr. Cole died in Philadelphia on August 14, 1922, after having practiced medicine for more than fifty years.

The third African-American woman to become a doctor was Susan Smith McKinney Steward. She was born Susan Maria Smith in 1847 in New York City. She later married twice, to a Mr. McKinney and a Mr. Steward, whose names she took. She graduated valedictorian of her class from the New York Medical College for Women in 1870. This school, which taught homeopathic medicine along with basic anatomy and physiology, had been founded by another pioneering woman of medicine, Dr. Clemence Sophia Lozier. Dr. Lozier and Dr. Steward become lifelong friends. During her forty-eight years of practice, Dr. Steward helped to found a hospital, served on the staff of a medical college, and was active in local medical societies and in the women's suffrage movement.

Many black women doctors probably slipped from history unknown. This might have been the case with Annie Elizabeth "Bessie" Delaney, one of the first black women dentists. But she saved her place in history when she and her sister, Sarah, wrote a best-selling book in 1993, when they were more than one hundred years old. *Having Our Say* illustrated the struggles of young professional black women in New York City during the 1920s and 1930s.

Along with those recorded by historians, there were no doubt many other fine African-American women doctors who remained unrecognized by the world at large.

Emeline Horton Cleveland

The First Woman Doctor to Perform Major Surgery

1829–1878

As a college student, Emeline Horton felt called to be a missionary, as did her childhood friend and college boyfriend, Giles Butler Cleveland. The two young people, while attending Oberlin College in Ohio, planned to marry and then go off to foreign lands. Giles was studying theology so that he could become a Presbyterian minister; Emeline discovered a medical school for women that had a program for medical missionaries. Giles did become a minister, and Emeline became a doctor. Giles soon fell ill, however, and they could not travel and fulfill their dreams of becoming missionaries. Instead, Dr. Emeline Horton Cleveland set up a medical practice to support their family and became one of the greatest of the early women surgeons in America.

Emeline Horton Cleveland was born on September 22, 1829, in Ashford, Connecticut. Her parents, Chauncey and Amanda Horton, had nine children, of whom Emeline was the third. In 1831, the Horton family moved to a farm in Madison County, New York. There, young Emeline had to help with farm and household chores as well as attend the school that her father set up on the farm. He hired a private teacher to come and hold classes for the Horton children.

When she was still quite young, Emeline herself became a schoolteacher, and saved the money she earned from teaching to pay for her education at Oberlin College. She was able to enroll at Oberlin in the autumn of 1850. Giles was also at Oberlin, in the Theological Seminary. They fell in love and began to dream of a life together as missionaries.

Meanwhile, Emeline learned something important in a letter from Sarah J. Hale, the editor of *Godey's Lady's Book,* one of the leading women's magazines of the 1800s. Hale told Emeline of a new medical school for women that had a program for training women doctors to serve as missionaries—the Female (later Woman's) Medical College of Pennsylvania.

In 1853, Giles graduated from the seminary and Emeline graduated from college. He found a church position in the Oneida Valley of New York State. She immediately enrolled in the Female Medical College. On March 8, 1854, while still a medical student, she married Giles Cleveland. She was awarded an M.D. degree in 1855.

The Clevelands' plans already were going awry. Giles had developed health problems, and they had to postpone their dream of becoming missionaries. Dr. Cleveland set up a medical practice in the Oneida Valley, but the Female Medical College wanted her to come back and teach anatomy. She tried this for the fall term of 1856, and did such a good job that she was invited to become professor of anatomy and histology (the study of tissues). She accepted, and the Clevelands moved to Philadelphia, where Giles found a post as a teacher. Then, Giles suffered another serious illness during the winter of 1857-1858 that left him partially paralyzed. He could no longer work. It was now up to Dr. Cleveland to support them both.

Dr. Ann Preston, a professor at the medical college, and other Quaker women of Philadelphia had plans for Dr. Cleveland. The Quakers had set up the Female Medical College because they believed that women had the right to be treated by women doctors, and regular medical schools refused to admit women. Now the women medical students could not get training with real patients, because the hospitals of Philadelphia refused to allow women medical students on their wards or in their clinics. Dr. Preston and the Quaker women decided that they must establish their own hospital for women and children. They looked about for someone to serve as its chief resident and chose Dr. Cleveland.

Dr. Preston wanted the new hospital's chief resident to have the finest training. The most advanced medicine at that time was in Europe. In 1860, Dr. Preston and her Quaker supporters sent Dr. Cleveland to Paris to study obstetrics and gynecological surgery. After completing her formal training in 1861, Dr. Cleveland then toured hospitals and attended lectures in Paris and London to learn all she could about hospital administration.

In 1862, she took on the job of chief resident of the Woman's Hospital of Philadelphia. During the seven years that she held this post, she set up training programs for nurses and for nurses' aides. In addition, she became a renowned surgeon. She performed daring and sophisticated operations, removing ovarian tumors and doing other major abdominal surgery. Not only was she the chief resident, a professor at the Woman's Medical College, and in private practice, but in 1865 she also gave birth to a son, her only child. He grew up to become a doctor like his mother. Dr. Cleveland was a woman who had it all and could do it all—wife, mother, and successful professional.

In 1872, Ann Preston died, and Dr. Cleveland succeeded her friend as dean of the Woman's Medical College. But the strain of her busy life was beginning to take a toll on her health. In 1874, she resigned. By then, Dr. Cleveland was one of the most highly respected physicians in Pennsylvania. Because of her achievements, women became more accepted by the male medical profession. Some male doctors even came to consult with Dr. Cleveland on their difficult cases. In 1878, The Pennsylvania Hospital hired her as gynecologist for its department for the insane, making Dr. Cleveland one of the first women doctors hired by a major public institution.

Her brilliant career, however, was about to come to an early end. At age forty-nine, Dr. Cleveland contracted tuberculosis (TB). Today, TB is treated with powerful antibiotics. But in the 1870s, TB was still a major killer with no known cure. Dr. Cleveland died on December 8, 1878, leaving behind her invalid husband and their son. One of her final requests was that she be buried in Philadelphia's Fair Hill Cemetery next to her colleague and friend, Dr. Preston.

Mary Harris Thompson

Founder of
Women's Hospital
and Medical School

1829–1895

T he evening of October 8, 1871, was warm and dry, like all the evenings in that year of drought. The new Woman's Hospital Medical College, the brainchild of Dr. Mary Harris Thompson, had begun its second year of classes only four days earlier. The students attending Chicago's first medical school for women eagerly looked forward to the opportunity to learn how to treat the sick. But a great disaster was about to interrupt their plans.

Shortly after 9:00 P.M., a red glow lit the sky to the south and west. A fire that had started in a barn behind the house of Mr. and Mrs. Patrick O'Leary was spreading rapidly, out of control. Flames, fed by the city's wooden houses and sidewalks and hay-filled barns, set one building after another ablaze. Panic broke out as families fled on foot or in horse-drawn wagons with their children and livestock. A strong wind whipped the flames into a virtual wall of fire that roared north across the Chicago River, destroying everything in its path—including Dr. Thompson's medical school and the hospital with which it was associated.

But Dr. Thompson had no time for self-pity. Thousands of injured and dying people filled the city, and Dr. Thompson and her staff set up an emergency hospital to care for them. The students settled into an old house and continued their studies. And once the emergency was over, Dr. Thompson and her supporters set about rebuilding the hospital and medical school in even larger quarters. Eventually, the medical school became part of Northwestern University.

Mary Harris Thompson was born on April 15, 1829, into a large family in Washington County, New York. All her life, Mary loved to learn. As a girl, she taught herself Latin and mathematics. When she was older, she attended a Methodist academy in Vermont and then a school in Fort Edward, New York. While she was away at school, her father, who owned part of an iron mine, had business problems. He no longer could afford to pay her tuition, and so Mary began serving as an instructor to pay for her education. She expected to become a schoolteacher in Vermont, and to prepare for this, she decided to study anatomy and physiology at the New England Female Medical College in Boston. It was common for women who were not training to become doctors to attend classes at the early female medical schools, since these lectures were one of the few available sources of information about their own bodies.

After a short time, Mary Thompson became fascinated by medicine. She went to New York City to intern with Elizabeth and Emily Blackwell, two of the first women doctors in America, at their New York

Infirmary for Women and Children. She completed her studies at the New England Female Medical College and received an M.D. degree in 1863.

She then had to decide where to set up her practice. It was difficult for women doctors to attract patients. There already were women doctors in Boston, New York, and Philadelphia, and she did not want to compete with them. She decided to seek opportunity in a boom town to the west—Chicago.

When Dr. Thompson arrived in Chicago, the Civil War was under way. She became active in the United States Sanitary Commission, a private organization created in 1861 to operate hospitals, distribute food, clothing, and medicine, and care for both Union and Confederate soldiers. Many of her first patients were poverty-striken wives and children of Union soldiers, and she soon decided that Chicago needed a hospital for women and children similar to the hospitals in Boston and New York City. With the help of a local clergyman, funds were raised for the Chicago Hospital for Women and Children, which opened in May 1865.

Dr. Thompson, with her lifelong love of learning, was anxious to receive more medical training. Outside of the schools established for women, few medical schools would accept female students. She applied to Rush Medical College, but was turned down because she was a woman. Then, in 1869, the Chicago Medical College agreed to admit her and two other women. Dr. Thompson received her diploma in 1870. The other women still had more courses to complete when the male students rebelled at the idea of allowing them to continue with their studies, and they were forced to leave.

This incident led Dr. Thompson and sympathetic male professors at the college to conclude that a women's medical school was needed in Chicago and that it should be affiliated with the Chicago Hospital for Women and Children. The Woman's Hospital Medical College opened

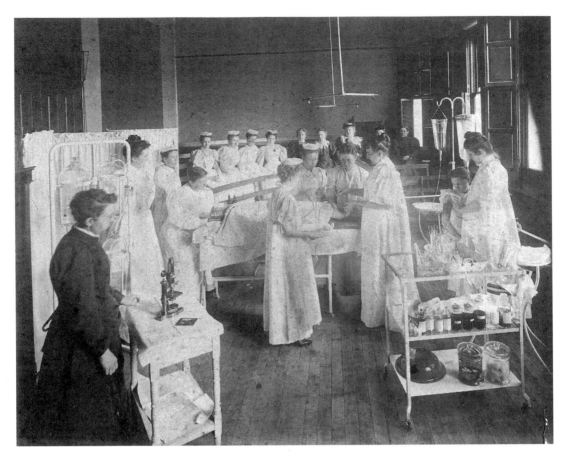

At the Northwestern University Woman's Medical School, women were trained in medicine during the late 1800s.

in 1870. Dr. Thompson served as professor of hygiene. The following year, the school and hospital burned to the ground in the Great Chicago Fire, but it was rebuilt and renamed the Woman's Medical College in 1879. In 1891, it became the Northwestern University Woman's Medical School.

During this time, Dr. Thompson also was building a reputation as one of the greatest surgeons in the Midwest. She began as a general surgeon, then specialized in abdominal surgery. Her skill, patience, and kindness eventually won her the admiration and acceptance of the local

male physicians, who were at first very hostile toward her. She was not only admitted to the Chicago Medical Society, but served as its vice-president from 1881 to 1882.

Chicago remained Dr. Thompson's home for the rest of her life. She died there of a cerebral hemorrhage on May 21, 1895. The hospital she founded was then renamed the Mary Thompson Hospital in her honor. As an enduring memorial, in 1905 the hospital presented to the Art Institute of Chicago a bust of Dr. Thompson by the renowned American sculptor, Daniel Chester French, whose works include the magnificent statue of Abraham Lincoln in the Lincoln Memorial in Washington, D.C.

Mary Harris Thompson

Marie Elizabeth Zakrzewska

Founder of the New England Hospital for Women and Children

1829–1902

Marie Zakrzewska dreamed of leaving Europe to find opportunity and freedom in America. Like so many immigrants in the mid-1800s, she landed in New York City with very little money. She couldn't even speak English. But she was not afraid to work, and work hard she did, taking up knitting to support herself. She also was not afraid to pursue her dream of becoming a doctor. She sought out Elizabeth Blackwell, the first woman doctor of modern medicine. With Blackwell's encouragement, Zakrzewska learned to speak English, obtained a medical degree, doctored destitute immigrants in the slums of New York and Boston, and went on to found a teaching hospital that educated two generations of women physicians.

Marie E. Zakrzewska was born in Berlin, Germany, on September 6, 1829, the first of six children born to Martin Ludwig and Frederika

Zakrzewska. Marie's father was descended from Polish landowners who lost their property after parts of Poland were partitioned, or divided, by Prussia and Russia in 1793. Her mother was descended from the Gypsy Lombardi tribe. Marie's father became an officer in the Prussian army and also worked as a government official.

When Marie was eight years old, she was sent to a girl's school. Although she was bright and a good student, school days were not happy for young Marie. She was plain looking, had a large nose, and was not at all popular with the other girls. As a result, she was very lonely.

Meanwhile, Martin Ludwig's superiors came to regard his political views as too liberal, and he lost his job. His liberal views, however, did not extend to the education of his daughter. When she was thirteen, he insisted she leave school and learn to do housework like all good German girls.

In order to support the family after Martin Ludwig lost his job, Frederika Zakrzewska enrolled at a school for midwives at a Berlin hospital. For several months, Marie lived with her mother at the hospital and became intensely interested in medicine. She began to read medical books on her own and even assisted her mother at childbirths. She couldn't wait to go to the midwife school herself. Finally, when she was twenty years old, she was admitted to the school and became an outstanding student, graduating in 1851. One of the professors, Dr. Joseph Hermann Schmidt, had made her his assistant and in 1852, insisted she become chief midwife and a professor. Unfortunately, Dr. Schmidt died within a week after Marie was promoted. She was left alone to fight opponents who felt that at age twenty-two she was much too young for such responsibility.

Marie resigned six months later, but the promise held out by the New World already was beginning to bring hope to Marie's life. She had heard of a women's medical college in Philadelphia. In the spring of

1853, she and a younger sister sailed to the United States. They were joined by another sister that fall. The three Zakrzewska sisters supported themselves by knitting.

Marie was determined to study medicine. At the time, Dr. Blackwell had gained fame as the first woman doctor and had opened a dispensary, or clinic, for poor women and children, most of them immigrants. Marie managed to be introduced to Dr. Blackwell and started helping out at the dispensary. Dr. Blackwell was impressed with Marie's intelligence and ability. Through Dr. Blackwell, arrangements were made for Marie to attend the Cleveland Medical College (now the medical school of Case Western Reserve University). A group of women's rights supporters raised money to pay her tuition. In 1856, she graduated and became Dr. Zakrzewska. She was one of six women doctors graduated from the Cleveland Medical College—including Elizabeth Blackwell's sister Emily—before it closed its doors to women.

Armed with her M.D. degree, Dr. Zakrzewska headed back to New York City and opened an office in Dr. Blackwell's residence. Along with the Blackwell sisters, she dreamed of opening a hospital for women and children. Dr. Zak, as she affectionately came to be called, raised funds in Philadelphia, Boston, and New York. On May 1, 1857, the New York Infirmary for Women and Children officially opened. Elizabeth Blackwell worked as a physician; Emily Blackwell, as the skilled surgeon. Dr. Zak was the obstetrician, resident physician, and general manager. She impressed everyone with her ability to work long hours, often rising at 5:30 A.M. and working until 11:30 P.M.

In 1859, another opportunity came her way. She was offered and accepted the post of professor of obstetrics and diseases of women and children at the New England Female Medical College in Boston. Unfortunately, this experience did not turn out as well as she had hoped. The college had low educational standards, and Dr. Zak's standards were very high. She believed that medical students should have a good general education and that medicine should have a solid scientific foundation. Her views were not shared by the founder and owner of the school, Samuel Gregory. Relations between them became increasingly strained, and Dr. Zak resigned in 1862.

With the backing of local women supporters, Dr. Zak then founded the New England Hospital for Women and Children. In her view, the most important task of the hospital was to aid in training women doctors and nurses while providing the best possible care for needy women and children. Dr. Zak had a great sympathy for the poor, and had been providing care to the needy herself from the time she first arrived in Boston. Under her expert supervision, the young women in training not only observed operations and births, but also the host of diseases—typhoid, diphtheria, and tuberculosis—that plagued the residents of the tenements.

Dr. Zak devoted the rest of her life to the New England Hospital, directing its activities, helping it grow, and overseeing its move to new and larger quarters in nearby Roxbury. Many of the best women doctors served their internships at the New England Hospital, and many believed that Dr. Zak was the greatest force in insuring the early success of women doctors in America.

Dr. Zak retired in 1899. Her health deteriorated due to cardiovascular disease. She died of a stroke three years later, on May 12, 1902. With typical forethought and organization, she had planned her funeral and written her obituary, which was read at the memorial service. And her legacy lived on in the women doctors she inspired. "I cannot measure how much I owe to her skillful, energetic, practical instruction as a physician when I was a student . . . ;" wrote one women doctor at the Hospital for Children in San Francisco, "neither can I measure the strength, courage, and hope which her bright example has given me throughout my life."

Emily Jennings Stowe

First Woman Licensed to Practice Medicine in Canada

1831–1903

anada was a frontier land experiencing both booming growth and political turmoil in the early 1830s, when Emily Jennings Stowe was growing up. When Emily was six years old, a rebellion broke out against British rule. The Dominion of Canada was not created until 1867, when Emily was thirty-six years old. During her lifetime, she witnessed many important events in Canadian history; she also created part of that history. Emily Stowe surmounted overwhelming odds to become the first woman licensed to practice medicine in Canada, and one of the first leaders of Canada's women's rights movement.

Emily Jennings was born in May 1831 in South Norwich, Upper Canada (now Ontario). Like many young ladies of that time who were able to get an education, she became a schoolteacher. She made history in the field of education in 1852 by becoming one of Canada's first female school principals.

In 1856, she married a dentist named John Stowe. The Stowes had three children—two sons and a daughter. But Emily Stowe longed for something more. She wanted to be a doctor. She came from a Quaker background, and Quakers were at the forefront of social reform. They wanted to see slavery abolished in the United States. They believed that women should have the right to vote and should have equal opportunities with men, including the right to a medical education. John also supported Emily's desire to become a doctor.

She began to search for a medical school, but no medical school in Canada would even consider admitting a woman. Emily Stowe arranged for a relative to help John with the children, and she set out for the New York Medical College and Hospital for Women, a homeopathic school in New York City. She graduated in 1867 and set up a medical practice in Toronto.

At first, this pioneering woman doctor had a difficult life. She drove her horse-drawn buggy to call on patients, who often paid her as little as fifty cents a visit. Then the male doctors of Toronto declared that she was practicing medicine illegally. Only doctors who were members of the Ontario College of Physicians and Surgeons could practice medicine, they said. This raised an insurmountable problem. No one could become a member of this professional organization unless they had graduated from a Canadian medical school. Since women were not admitted into Canadian medical schools, Dr. Stowe never would be able to practice medicine legally.

She ignored them. The male doctors had her fined and threatened to throw her in jail, but she fought them at every turn. In the end, she won. She was allowed to take one session at a Toronto medical school.

The male students constantly harassed her, but she endured it all, and in 1880 she was licensed as Canada's first official woman doctor.

Not wanting other women medical students to suffer the way she had, she began a crusade for women's education. She and other women's rights activists pressured the University of Toronto into admitting women undergraduates. The university would not agree to admit women medical students, and so Dr. Stowe and a group of supporters helped organize the Ontario Medical College for Women, which was affiliated with the University of Toronto.

Dr. Stowe's efforts on behalf of women were not limited to medical education. She was a strong believer in women's suffrage. In 1877, she organized the first local suffrage organization in Canada, disguised with the name "The Women's Literary Club." Then, in 1893, she organized the Dominion Woman Suffrage Association and became its first president.

Dr. Stowe died in Toronto on April 30, 1903. The work she began was carried on by her daughter, Augusta. Augusta was the first woman to be educated at a Canadian medical school and the first to marry another doctor, J. B. Gullen. She practiced under the name Dr. Augusta Stowe-Gullen.

Mary Edward Walker

First Woman U.S. Army Surgeon

1832–1919

When she was sixteen years old, Mary Walker promised her father that she would never bind herself into the unhealthy, tight-laced corsets that were fashionable at that time. She went much further than that; she took to wearing trousers, a practice that in the mid-1800s scandalized both women and men. She also took to wearing the uniform of a male Army officer, a right she felt was hers after she was appointed the first woman surgeon in the U.S. Army.

Mary Edward Walker was born on November 26, 1832, in Oswego Town, New York, one of five girls and a boy in the family of Vesta and

Alvah Walker. Her father, Alvah, worked the family farm but also had taught himself the art of medicine. Doctors in that time were not required to go through any standard type of training. Some served apprenticeships, others were self-taught. Given those conditions, Alvah Walker was as good a doctor as any in rural New York State.

Alvah Walker thought the fashions of the times were immoral and unhygienic. The well-dressed woman was expected to wear a dozen petticoats under a floor-length skirt and to have her waist and upper body laced into a tight-fitting corset. The corsets were so tight that women had trouble breathing. At the slightest exertion, a woman might faint for lack of oxygen, which helped support the notion that women were weak and delicate creatures. Mary readily embraced her father's views on feminine fashion. She also thought this fashion was an expression of a hypocritical refusal to acknowledge that women had legs. Women, with their legs hidden under billowing skirts, were expected to glide along as if by magic. Not only did Mary reject wearing corsets but, as a teenager, she was determined to acknowledge that she had legs.

At about that time, a woman named Amelia Bloomer unveiled a new costume for women. It consisted of a knee-length skirt worn over puffy trousers. The press quickly nick-named the pants "bloomers" and the women who wore them "bloomer girls." The leaders of the new movement to win the vote for women adopted this freer fashion, as did Mary Walker.

The women's suffrage movement was getting under way when Mary reached adulthood. The leaders of the women's movement had started to succeed in opening the medical profession to women. When Mary decided to become a doctor like her father, she was able to gain admission to the Syracuse Medical College, from which she graduated in 1853.

At medical school, she met Albert Miller of Rome, New York, and soon after graduating, they married. The two set up practice in Rome, but Mary never took his name. The couple separated in 1859 and were divorced in 1869.

Meanwhile, the Civil War broke out, and Mary Walker was anxious to serve. She applied for appointment as a Union Army surgeon. Rejected, she had to be content working as an unpaid hospital volunteer. Undaunted and unauthorized, she headed for the battlefields of Virginia, where she volunteered in field hospitals. In 1863, she was appointed an assistant surgeon with the Army of the Cumberland, and served at Chattanooga, Tennessee, when the casualties from the fighting at Chickamauga began to pour in.

The men were amazed when the short, thin, and frail-looking woman showed up in the uniform of a lieutenant, the rank she had been given. Apparently, Dr. Walker never succeeded in winning their hearts and minds, and some questioned her competency.

Historical records show that surgeons serving during the Civil War often were poorly qualified. Also, surgical treatment available at that time was primitive and not much more advanced than what was available in the Middle Ages. Most operations were amputations, and because of the pain and trauma involved, the mark of a good surgeon was speed. In most cases, Civil War surgeons had access to chloroform or ether, so their patients could be put to sleep while the surgeon dug out a bullet, or amputated an arm or leg shattered by a Minnie Ball. But many of the patients later died of infections caused by unsterile instruments and bandages. The doctors had yet to learn about the causes of infection.

In addition to performing services for the Union troops, Walker often would venture outside the Union lines to treat patients in the civilian population, who suffered from a range of ills, from toothaches to complications of childbirth. Many were grateful and recalled her as being kind and warmhearted. But some of the Union soldiers thought that because she crossed into enemy territory she was a spy.

On one of her trips to treat the townspeople, Dr. Walker was captured by Confederate troops. She was held as a prisoner of war in Richmond, Virginia, for four months, then released in a prisoner exchange. From then until the end of the war she served first as supervisor of a hospital for women prisoners, then as head of an orphanage in Tennessee. In 1865, she was given the Congressional Medal of Honor for Meritorious Service.

After the Civil War ended, Dr. Walker enjoyed several years of fame and took to the lecture circuit. In 1866, she was elected president of the National Dress Reform Association. She and Belva Lockwood promoted the cause of women's suffrage.

Dr. Walker, however, apparently had an attitude problem. While she was tough-minded, strong, and courageous, she could also be tactless and harsh. She was very much an individualist rather than a team player. In fact, she angered the leaders of the women's suffrage movement by asserting that a Constitutional amendment guaranteeing women the right to vote was nonsense. Women already had that Constitutional right by means of the Fourteenth Amendment, Dr. Walker asserted. She lobbied hard for passage in state legislatures of a measure making it illegal to deny women that Constitutional right. She called this her Crowning Constitutional Argument.

At the same time, she began to wear men's clothes all the time. Because of her views and her wardrobe, she was regarded as an eccentric and a perfect target for ridicule in the press. There were whispered insinuations about her sexual orientation. In 1917, the U.S. government concluded that her Medal of Honor had not been warranted and notified her that it was being taken away. With typical spunk, Dr. Walker informed Congress that she had been given two copies of the medal.

Mary Walker in a photograph taken by Matthew Brady

One she intended to wear every day, and the other she would wear on special occasions.

Dr. Walker continued to be highly visible in the halls of Congress almost until her death. In 1917, she took a fall down the steps of the Capitol and never fully recovered. She died on February 21, 1919, and was buried in the family plot in Oswego Town. Despite her shortcomings and the comments of her critics, Dr. Walker left the legacy of being the first woman military doctor in the United States.

Clara A. Swain

Pioneering Medical Missionary

1834–1910

When the British ladies of the Zenana Bible and Medical Mission went off in 1852 to convert the Hindu and Muslim women of India to Christianity, they encountered a problem of far more concern than the women's spiritual well-being. According to religious custom, Muslim women and some high-caste Hindus lived by the rules of purdah, which required that women be kept hidden from men. The women lived in zenanas, a part of the house set aside exclusively for women. Men were not allowed to enter. This practice created serious health-care problems for the women. All the doctors in India were male; therefore doctors never examined purdah women. Modesty would not allow it.

These Indian women bore children with only the aid of poorly trained midwives in highly unsanitary conditions. Many of the children died from diseases that could have been treated by a doctor, and many of the women, without access to good medical care, lived their lives as invalids. But all this began to change with the arrival in India of Clara Swain, the first woman doctor and medical missionary to "non-Christian lands." Not only did Dr. Swain treat the purdah women, she also began to train them as doctors to serve in the zenanas.

Clara A. Swain, the tenth and youngest child of John and Clarissa Swain, was born on July 18, 1834, in Elmira, New York, but grew up in Castile, New York. As a young girl, she loved to read. When she had finished reading all of her brothers' and sisters' books, she borrowed books from the neighbors. Her entire family encouraged her to learn and to teach. When she was fifteen years old, she went to live with an aunt in Michigan, where she taught school for a year. Then another aunt in Canandaigua, New York, invited her for a year of study at a local seminary. Clara stayed on to teach public school there for seven years.

Deep inside, Clara was not happy with teaching. She had discovered that she had a talent for healing when she had been called upon to care for sick friends and relatives. Gradually, the idea of becoming a doctor took hold. In 1865, when she was thirty-one years old, she began to train in medicine at the Castile Sanitarium, owned and operated by one of the earliest women doctors, Dr. Cordelia A. Greene. From 1866 to 1869, Clara attended the Woman's Medical College of Pennsylvania, earning the M.D. degree.

The atmosphere at the Castile Sanitarium suited Dr. Swain well. It was deeply spiritual, and so was she. At age nine, she had been moved by a Methodist preacher's sermon on evangelism, and the need to spread the Christian Gospel around the world. It was one of the most important—and controversial—ideas of Western civilization in the

1800s. Thousands of Protestant missionaries were sent to India, the Far East, and Africa. Dr. Swain was ready when the Woman's Foreign Missionary Society of the Methodist Episcopal Church asked the Woman's Medical College to help recruit a "lady physician" to serve a mission school and orphanage in the northwest Indian city of Bareilly.

A group of English women missionaries and male doctors at Bareilly were trying to give young women some medical training so they could work in the zenanas. Dr. Swain agreed to not only treat patients but also train Indian women. Her first class had 17 women, who listened to her lectures on anatomy, physiology, and drug treatments and accompanied her on her rounds to see patients. Dr. Swain's fame grew, and so did the number of her patients. In order to handle the work load, she needed a hospital and clinic where she could dispense medicine. She offered to buy land from the local ruler, the Nawab of Rampore.

The Nawab despised missionaries. Like many people in lands where there were Protestant missionaries, the Nawab resented the foreign interests the missionaries represented and the fact that missionaries usually considered Western religion and ways of life superior to local customs and values. The missionaries were there to change the native beliefs. However, he strongly supported the idea of women doctors to care for the purdah women, and he was impressed with the work of Dr. Swain. The Nawab donated the land on which Clara Swain built the first hospital in India for women, which opened in 1874.

Dr. Swain was respectful of the local customs. The hospital was designed to accommodate women of all religions and castes and to protect the privacy of women observing purdah. Nevertheless, Dr. Swain managed to uphold her evangelistic ideals. To every prescription she handed out, a Bible verse was attached.

During 1875, her practice grew to some two thousand patients. They came from as far away as Burma. The work load was crushing, and in early 1876, her health gave out. She returned home to Castile on furlough after five years of medical missionary service, but by early 1880, Dr. Swain was back in India again. She worked at the women's hospital in Bareilly until 1885, when the prince of an Indian state, the Rajah of Rajputana, invited Dr. Swain to be the physician to the women of his palace. She agreed on one condition—that she be free to carry on her evangelical activities. He agreed, and built a clinic and house for Dr. Swain. She not only tended the women of the palace, but often would ride off on her elephant to treat patients in outlying villages.

While Dr. Swain never gave up her Christian evangelistic ideals, she came to love and respect the Indian people and their customs. She became a close friend of the rajah's family. In 1896, when it was time for her to retire, the rajah, his wife, and children begged Dr. Swain to stay on with them in India. However, she decided to return to Castile, New York, where she remained until her death on December 25, 1910.

The British medical profession eventually opened to women and many British women doctors were then trained and sent to India. These women, in turn, helped open the universities and medical schools of India for the training of Indian women doctors.

Elizabeth Garrett Anderson

First British Woman Doctor

1836–1917

The British medical men in the mid-1800s were determined that no woman ever would be passed by a British medical examining board and licensed to practice medicine. But Elizabeth Garrett was determined to succeed. With a combination of charm, cunning, and sheer determination, she managed to get around every roadblock that the medical establishment threw in her path. She found a legal loophole and used it to become the first registered English woman doctor.

Elizabeth Garrett was born in London on June 9, 1836, to Newson and Louisa Garrett. In all, the Garretts had nine children and raised them in the family home at Aldeburgh, Suffolk, on the eastern coast of England. Newson Garrett was a well-to-do grain merchant, and the family lived quite comfortably.

Elizabeth was fortunate to know many famous people of the day. She attended a boarding school run by the aunts of the poet Robert Browning. Her best friend was Emily Davies, who was destined to open British universities to women. Elizabeth's own sister, Millicent Garrett Fawcett, would help win the vote for British women.

Although she lived at home, as proper young women were expected to do, until she was twenty-six years old, Elizabeth was exposed through her social contacts to many of the radical ideas of the day. For example, she was friendly with a group of women's rights leaders in London who were trying to get women access to "white-collar" employment. About the only work then available to somewhat educated women who had to earn a living was service as domestic companions or as governesses to children of the rich.

The great turning point in Elizabeth's life came in March 1859, when the women's employment rights group invited Dr. Elizabeth Blackwell to give a series of lectures on the medical education of women. Dr. Blackwell was the first woman doctor of modern times. She had been born in England, emigrated to the United States, and received her M.D. degree from a medical school in New York State. After meeting with Dr. Blackwell, Elizabeth Garrett was inspired to make her life's goal that of opening the British medical profession to women, and she would begin by becoming a doctor herself.

When she broke the news to her parents, her father strongly objected and her mother wept to think of the disgrace this would bring on the family name. Elizabeth was charming and attractive; why couldn't she just settle down and get married? But Elizabeth did not let her parents' reactions bother her. She was blessed with a good sense of humor, an easygoing disposition, and a very positive outlook on life. First, she persuaded her father not to stand in her way. Then, when he saw how the medical establishment had stacked the cards so unfairly against her, he became an active supporter of her struggle.

The situation was this: When Dr. Blackwell visited England in 1858, she had not yet become a United States citizen, so her name was placed on the British Medical Register, which had been recently established to protect the public from unqualified "doctors." This gave her the legal right to practice medicine in Great Britain. The medical establishment wanted to keep other women from doing the same. So a law was passed stating that no one could be placed on the Medical Register unless they had been licensed by a qualified examining board, such as a British university. Foreign degrees no longer would be accepted. The unspoken rule was that no woman would be able to take an examination with a British examining board, because British universities were closed to women.

Elizabeth Garrett was not about to be stopped by a technicality. Through friends of Dr. Blackwell, she was able to get a six-month contract as a nurse at Middlesex Hospital, one of the largest teaching hospitals in London. Once there, she used her good nature, tact, and intelligence to win over members of both the nursing and surgical staffs. Soon, she was observing surgical operations and following the doctors and medical students on their rounds. Unfortunately, the male students felt threatened by her talent and her ability to learn quickly. They circulated a petition for her removal, and she had to leave Middlesex Hospital.

Undaunted, she applied to the medical schools of the great universities of Oxford, Cambridge, London, St. Andrews, and Edinburgh. They all turned her down flat. Meanwhile, she and her father found the loophole through which she could enter the British Medical Register.

Another British medical group, called the Society of Apothecaries, granted a degree called the L.S.A. It was not as prestigious as an M.D., but holders of an L.S.A. were considered to be qualified physicians and so could be placed on the Medical Register. The society's charter said it would accept all qualified persons. It did not specify that they had to be male. The society reluctantly agreed that they could not refuse to admit Elizabeth once she had served an apprenticeship with a physician and gathered a specified number of certificates showing she had attended the required courses or had been tutored privately by qualified teachers. They believed that this would be impossible. How wrong they were.

By that time, Elizabeth had met many sympathetic physicians. She served an apprenticeship with and was privately tutored by several medical school professors, including a famous gynecologist at the University of Edinburgh, Sir James Simpson. All the while, she received encouragement from her friend, Emily Davies, her sister, Millicent, and their friends in the growing women's movement.

After more than five grueling years, Elizabeth Garrett returned to the Society of Apothecaries with all the requirements completed, and demanded membership. They still tried to keep her out, but legally they could not. In September 1865, she took the qualifying examinations, passed them easily, and in 1866, her name was entered in the Medical Register. However, because she did not have an M.D. degree, she had to be called "Miss" rather than "Doctor."

Miss Garrett opened a private practice in London, and many of her friends in the womens' movement became her patients. She also opened a clinic for poor women and children in a slum area of London. Eventually, the clinic became the New Hospital for Women, the first British hospital staffed by women doctors and nurses.

Miss Garrett was not finished; she wanted to be appointed to the staff of a regular hospital. She was able to accomplish this in 1869, when she applied for and was accepted as a consulting physician on the staff of the Shadwell Hospital for Children. There, she met the man she would marry, James George Skelton Anderson, an executive with the

Orient steamship line and a member of the hospital board.

Before she married she had one more item of business to conclude: earning an M.D. degree and the right to be called Doctor. In 1868, the University of Paris opened to women, and Miss Garrett enrolled in the medical school. By then, she had many highly placed supporters, including the Emperor Napoleon III. She took refresher courses in the basic sciences, shuttled across the English Channel between England and France, and in 1870, received her M.D. degree. She returned to England as Dr. Garrett.

That same year, she was elected for the first time to public office. A law recently had been passed that allowed women to serve on local school boards—even though women did not yet have the right to vote. The husbands of the women she treated at her New Hospital called on Dr. Garrett, urging her to run for a seat on the London school board. She did so and received the largest number of votes ever recorded in a London school board election.

The following year, 1871, she became Dr. Anderson when she married James Anderson. Despite the fears of her feminist friends that she would abandon her profession, she carried on her medical career while she raised a son and a daughter. In 1873, she became the first woman member of the British Medical Association. She joined the teaching staff of the London School of Medicine for Women, founded by Dr. Sophia Jex-Blake, and lectured there on medicine from 1875 to 1897. She also served as dean of the school from 1883 to 1903, when she retired from medicine. She moved with her husband back to her childhood home in Aldeburgh, which had been bequeathed to her by her father.

Soon after, Mr. Anderson was elected mayor of the town, and when he died in 1907, Dr. Anderson finished out his term. She then won election as mayor in her own right. This gave her the opportunity to put in place plans for a better sanitation system and better housing. All her

Elizabeth Garrett Anderson with her husband James G. Skelton Anderson

Elizabeth Garrett Anderson
97

life, Dr. Anderson had believed that it was better to maintain health than to try and cure illness, and the role of good sanitation was beginning to be recognized as key to this goal.

Dr. Anderson died on December 17, 1917, but her contributions lived after her. Not only was she the spiritual mother of the next generation of British women physicians, she was the physical mother of another great woman doctor. Her daughter, Dr. Louisa Garrett Anderson, helped open the field of military medicine to women doctors by organizing a field hospital on the front lines during World War I, a hospital that was managed by women.

Sophia Jex-Blake

Pioneer in British Women's Medical Education

1840–1912

Like many young women today, Sophia Jex-Blake could hardly wait until she was able to get a job and start earning money on her own. But Sophia was a young woman from a wealthy British family, and in the mid-1800s such a thing was unheard of. Sophia's desire to work for pay was just another in a long line of misdeeds, as far as her mother and father were concerned. They had regularly sent the high-spirited and temperamental Sophia off to boarding school, hoping the school could turn her into a proper Christian lady; that is, one who would be quiet and mannerly and live at home until a suitable man asked for her hand in marriage. But Sophia had ideas of her own, and once her mind was set on something, there was nothing that could stop her. Her fighting spirit eventually put her at the forefront of the struggle to open British medical schools and other institutions of higher learning to women. Although she faced overwhelming odds and hostile opponents, she won.

Sophia Jex-Blake was born on January 21, 1840, at Hastings, England, a town on the English Channel, south of London. Her father was an independently wealthy man, very conservative and very pious. Her mother was a nervous person and in delicate health. On hearing of Sophia's escapades, Sophia's mother often had to take to her bed. There was little the elder Jex-Blakes could do but disapprove of the behavior of their strong-willed daughter, who always did exactly as she wished. When Queen's College for Women opened in London, the eighteen-year-old Sophia wished to enroll. Not only did she go off to college, where she excelled in mathematics, but she took a job as a tutor—and accepted pay for her work. Her father promised to give her a fortune if she would just settle down and marry some suitable man. But Sophia wouldn't think of it. She was inspired by the women's rights leaders, who were crusading for a woman's right to higher education and the right to earn a decent living.

Things went from bad to worse between Sophia and her parents when she announced she was leaving for America. Nevertheless, off she sailed in 1865 to do a survey of colleges there. Sophia Jex-Blake's interest at the time was not in medicine but in higher education for women. When she arrived in the United States, however, she met Dr. Lucy Sewall and the other women doctors working at the New England Hospital for Women near Boston. Dr. Sewall became her personal physician and lifelong friend. Soon, Sophia Jex-Blake was deeply involved with the New England Hospital, working as secretary and medical records clerk. She never had been happier than she was working and socializing with the women doctors. She sent letters home to England imploring her mother to see life as she did. "Can't you understand," she wrote, "how refreshing it is to slip into the bright life of all these working people—working hard all day and then so ready for fun when work's over?"

It was only a matter of time before Sophia Jex-Blake decided to become a doctor. As usual, she wanted to do it her way. There were second- and third-rate medical colleges in the United States that would grant to degrees to anyone—even women—who could afford to pay. But Sophia wanted a university degree, and so she applied to Harvard. She received this reply: "There are no provisions for the education of women in any department of this University."

Meanwhile, in 1868, Elizabeth Blackwell, the first woman granted an M.D. degree in the United States, opened the Women's Medical College of the New York Infirmary, a high-quality medical school for women in New York City. Sophia Jex-Blake was one of its first students. It seemed as though she had found the right road to hard work and happiness, but it wasn't long before everything fell apart.

A letter came from England saying Mr. Jex-Blake was very ill and dying, and Sophia had to return home at once. When she left to board the ship that would take her back to England, she knew that she would not be returning to America; she would have to stay in England to help her mother. But, speaking like a prophet, Dr. Sewall told the unhappy Sophia that she was destined to open the British medical profession for herself and other women.

In 1869, Sophia Jex-Blake was ready to begin her campaign to accomplish that goal. She learned there were sympathetic professors at the University of Edinburgh in Scotland, so she applied to the medical school there. Eventually, the university agreed to allow Sophia and four other women to study medicine, but in separate classes from the men.

Things went well enough until one of the women medical students, Edith Pechey, took first place on a chemistry exam, and thus deserved a prestigious scholarship. But the scholarship was awarded instead to a male who had done less well on the exam.

The Scottish newspapers published this story, which set off a storm of protest throughout Great Britain, with letters-to-the-editor protesting the university's unsporting action. Opinion at the university, perhaps in response, turned against the women. Male students, supported by some male faculty members, engaged in a campaign of harassment designed to get rid of the women. Sophia Jex-Blake led the campaign to have the women stay. She was an outspoken activist, her dark eyes flashing with anger every time she met the next outrage. First, it became increasingly difficult to find professors who would teach the women. Then, the women were denied clinical training at the Royal Free Infirmary. The whole situation came to a head with a riot outside a building where the women were to take exams.

Again, public opinion was aroused and newspaper stories appeared all over Great Britain. A citizen's committee to secure medical education for women was organized, with Jex-Blake at its head. Jex-Blake, the committee, the university, and some of the faculty became entangled in complex legal actions that left Sophia with a huge debt in court fees. After a long series of rulings and appeals, in 1873 the courts found that the women medical students could not take the examinations that would lead to their licensing as physicians because the university was wrong to admit them in the first place.

Jex-Blake then took her cause to Parliament, which in 1876 passed a bill enabling all universities in what was then called the United Kingdom and Ireland to grant degrees to women. Meanwhile, unable to gain entrance to an existing medical school, Jex-Blake started her own. The London School of Medicine for Women opened in 1874, and Dr.

Elizabeth Garrett Anderson, the first British woman doctor, joined the teaching staff.

In 1877, Jex-Blake received her M.D. degree from the University of Berne in Switzerland. That same year, she went around the restrictive rules in England, and passed examinations by the Irish College of Physicians, allowing her to practice medicine in Britain.

The long political battle had turned the tide of public opinion in favor of women doctors, but many people—even those within her own camp—objected to the combative style and tone Jex-Blake had taken while leading the struggle. They regarded her as very difficult to get along with. So in 1883, it was not she, but Dr. Anderson, who was named dean of the medical school that Jex-Blake had founded.

Dr. Jex-Blake, who had started to practice medicine in Edinburgh, cut all ties to the London school and founded first a hospital and then a women's medical school in Edinburgh. She retired from medicine in 1899 and died on January 7, 1912.

Although she and the British medical establishment were bitter enemies while the struggle to admit women was going on, in later years they more or less made peace. A portrait of Dr. Sophia Jex-Blake was hung in the Royal Society of Medicine, and when the University of Edinburgh finally agreed to admit women in 1894, she was an invited and warmly welcomed guest at the proceedings.

Mary Putnam Jacobi

Leader in the Study of Women's Health

1842–1906

Everyone assumed that Mary Putnam would become a writer, perhaps a great one. She had begun to write at the age of six, and at seventeen sold her first short story to the *Atlantic Monthly*. In addition, she came from one of America's great publishing families; her father founded G. P. Putnam & Sons. But young Mary had another, even deeper interest—science, especially medical science. Instead of becoming a great fiction writer, she became a great woman physician, perhaps the greatest of her generation. She helped to introduce scientific principles to the practice of medicine and turned her writing talents to the service of medical science.

Mary Corinna Putnam was born on August 31, 1842, in London, England, where her parents were staying while her father, George Palmer

Putnam, set up a London branch of his publishing business. Mary was the first of eleven children born to George and Victorine Putnam.

The Putnams returned to America in 1848 and lived in various suburban areas outside New York City. Mary's early school lessons were taught by her mother, and Mary also spent a year at a private school in Yonkers and two years at a public school in Manhattan. All this time, her interest in everything to do with science was growing stronger.

When she was eighteen years; old, Mary announced that she wanted to attend medical school. Reluctantly, Mr. and Mrs. Putnam agreed, but only if the medical school was in New York City. By then, Elizabeth Blackwell and others had begun to open the profession to women. Still, most medical schools automatically rejected any application from a female. All the medical schools in New York City turned Mary down. Finally, she found a school that would accept her—the New York College of Pharmacy. She graduated from that school in 1863, becoming the first American woman pharmacist. She was not content with this, however; she wanted to be a doctor.

The Civil War temporarily led her to postpone her plans. First, her brother became ill with malaria at an army camp near New Orleans, and she went there to nurse him. Then her sister, who was teaching newly freed slaves in South Carolina, came down with typhoid, and so Mary went there too. She travelled alone on routes that took her very close to enemy territory. Although she was only five feet tall, Mary Putnam was sturdy and strong-willed. Through her actions, she made the point that these Civil War journeys were certainly more dangerous than a trip to Philadelphia would be to attend the newly founded Female (Woman's) Medical College of Pennsylvania.

Her parents relented, but her father, particularly, had many misgivings about her career choice ". . . I am proud of your abilities and am willing that you should apply them even to the repulsive pursuit . . . of medical education," he wrote. But he continued, ". . . if you must be a doctor and a philosopher, be an attractive and an agreeable one."

Because she had a pharmacy degree, Mary was able to get through medical school in one year, becoming an M.D. in 1864. She then served an internship under Dr. Marie Zakrzewska at the New England Hospital for Women and Children in Boston. Dr. Zak and other pioneering women doctors had made great progress in raising the standards of medicine and medical education. They learned and taught all the medical knowledge available at the time. But to the scientifically minded Dr. Putnam, this was not enough.

Medical treatments then were mainly a matter of trial and error. Doctors were not yet able to diagnose many specific diseases. For example, internal ailments, from indigestion to colon cancer, were called "dyspepsia" or "obstruction of the bowels" and treated with purgatives, powerful laxatives or chemicals that cause vomiting. Doctors viewed pneumonia and other infectious diseases as ailments that had to be driven from the body by bleeding the patient as well as giving them purgatives. If a treatment failed or succeeded, doctors had no idea why. Usually if patients recovered it was because of "benign neglect," the failure to administer any of these awful treatments, and instead let the patients get well on their own.

But medicine was on the brink of revolutionary change. In Europe, scientists were beginning to discover that germs cause infectious diseases. In Paris, Louis Pasteur discovered that bacteria spread disease. In Glasgow, Scotland, surgeon Joseph Lister realized that pus was caused by bacteria, and that by using carbolic acid to kill germs in the operating room, he could prevent infections in surgical wounds.

Dr. Putnam began to wonder whether medicine was the right profession for her. Perhaps she should be a laboratory scientist instead. At any rate, she decided that she wanted to study at the great University of

Paris, where doctors were using new instruments, such as the stethoscope, to hear heartbeats, and the microscope, to view tiny, disease-causing germs.

There was just one problem. The University of Paris did not admit women. Dr. Putnam did not let this stop her. She consulted with other pioneering women doctors and devised a strategy for gaining acceptance. First, she went to Paris and found sympathetic professors who allowed her to follow the medical students on rounds, attend surgeries, and borrow medical books. She then learned that the French government was in favor of admitting women to the medical school. Dr. Putnam applied and, in 1868, became the first woman ever admitted to the University of Paris medical school. She soon was followed by Englishwoman Elizabeth Garrett Anderson, who actually graduated first.

While Dr. Putnam was in Paris, funds for her education were in short supply. G. P. Putnam & Sons was going through difficult financial times. Dr. Putnam earned money by writing articles for American newspapers and magazines. It was a perilous time in Paris. The French were defeated by German troops in the Franco-Prussian War of 1870-1871. Paris surrendered to Prussian troops who had laid siege to the city and cut off its food supplies. Before the surrender, starving Parisians ate anything—even rats—to stay alive. Mary Putnam sent back front line reports on the conditions in Paris to American publications.

The war ended in 1871 and Mary Putnam received her M.D. degree from the university. She returned to New York City to become a professor at the new Women's Medical College founded by her friend, Dr. Elizabeth Blackwell, at the New York Infirmary. Dr. Putnam was determined to raise the standard of medical education for women, but she soon earned the reputation of being an impossibly tough teacher. The students were outraged because the material she covered in her lectures was too difficult for them to understand. Worse yet, she dared to ask the students questions in class. She also opposed the practice of teaching the same material two years in a row so that what a student missed the first time around they might get the second time. Instead, she wanted graded courses with different material taught during each session, beginning with the easiest material and progressing to the more difficult. She wanted her students to be better prepared.

Her ideas are standard educational practice today, but in the late 1800s they were radical. Dr. Emily Blackwell, who had been running the school since her sister Elizabeth had gone to England, did not agree that American schools needed this "French" approach. Dr. Putnam threatened to resign, but Elizabeth Blackwell wrote from England, counseling Dr. Putnam to be patient and stay on. She did so—for nearly twenty years. During that time, she saw many of her ideas on medical education put into practice.

Meanwhile, Mary Putnam met the love of her life, Dr. Abraham Jacobi, a leading pediatrician of the day, who opposed the popular notion that many infants died from teething. He argued that diseases killed babies, not the natural process of cutting teeth. He also campaigned to have abandoned newborns placed in foster homes with foster parents, rather than in foundling hospitals, where they inevitably died. Dr. Putnam and Dr. Jacobi met when she was invited to join the New York County Medical Society, of which Dr. Jacobi was president. They were married on July 22, 1873, and had three children. Only one child, their daughter Marjorie, survived to adulthood.

Despite the losses in her personal life, the career of Dr. Mary Putnam Jacobi thrived. She became an attending physician at the New York Infirmary and helped establish a pediatric clinic at Mt. Sinai Hospital. She was a visiting physician at St. Mark's Hospital and a lecturer to both men and women at the New York Post-Graduate Medical School. She also was active in the women's suffrage movement.

A high point in both her scientific career and her efforts to win rights for women came in 1876, when she won Harvard University's Boylston Prize, an award that carried great prestige. The winning work was her report, "The Question of Rest for Women during Menstruation." A prevalent attitude among male doctors was that menstruation produced severe weakness in all women, not unlike an illness. This idea contributed to the myth that women were an inferior sex. To refute this, Mary Jacobi carried out research on more than a thousand women and found that they were not incapacitated by menstrual periods and in fact felt better when they carried on with their normal work. The Harvard faculty had a very prejudiced attitude toward women, and the only reason she had a chance of winning the Boylston Prize was that the essays were submitted anonymously. The judges had no idea that the study had been done by a woman.

Mary Putnam Jacobi's dedication to medical science endured to the end of her life. Medical specialties were beginning to develop by the early 1900s, and she became interested in the specialty of neurology. Ironically, a neurological condition ended her life. One morning, this vigorous, energetic woman awoke with a severe headache. Morning after morning, the pain stabbed through her head. As a doctor, she knew something was very wrong. She diagnosed her own condition as a rare brain tumor. She knew it would be fatal, yet she calmly and scientifically wrote her own case history, detailing the progression of her condition, "Meningeal Tumor Compressing the Cerebellum." She died on June 10, 1906. At her memorial service at the New York Academy of Medicine, some of the most famous doctors in the world came to praise and honor her.

Mary Eliza Mahoney

*First
African-American
Graduate Nurse*

1845–1926

At the time Mary Mahoney was born, the abolition movement to end slavery was becoming a major political force in the United States. The year she turned twenty, the American Civil War ended and the Thirteenth Amendment to the United States Constitution was passed, abolishing slavery. The next great task for African Americans was the struggle for social and political equality. Mary Mahoney made major contributions to this effort. She became the first African American to graduate from a school of nursing, and she devoted the rest of her life to the nursing profession, and, in particular, to raising the status of black nurses.

Mary Eliza Mahoney, born on April 16, 1845, in Boston, Massachusetts, was the first of three children in the family of Charles and Mary Jane Mahoney. Historians have found few details about Mahoney's early life. Her parents made their way from North Carolina, a slave state, to Massachusetts, a free state. The family apparently did not have much money, because Mary had to work until she was thirty-three before she could enter nursing school.

When she was a teenager, she became interested in the brand-new profession of nursing. The first school of nursing had been established in London by the world-famous Florence Nightingale when Mary Mahoney was fifteen years old. Fortunately for Mahoney and for nursing, Boston was the home of the New England Hospital for Women and Children, where she went to work as a maid, cook, and washerwoman. The New England Hospital had been established by some of the first women doctors in the United States, and in the early 1870s became the first U.S. institution to offer nurses' training. In 1873 the first trained American nurse graduated. The pioneering medical women who founded the hospital had suffered a great deal of discrimination in their struggle to become doctors, so they were sympathetic to a young, bright, black woman wanting to become a nurse.

In 1878, Mahoney was one of about forty women to enter nurses' training at the New England Hospital. The academic standards there were very high. The courses were tough and the days were long—from 6:00 A.M. to 9:00 P.M. The student nurses spent twelve months gaining experience on the maternity, medical, and surgical wards and four months of private duty in patients' homes. They also attended lectures by the hospital's founder, Dr. Marie Zakrzewska. Only four of the forty students in Mahoney's entering class made it through this course of study, and she was one of them. She was awarded her nursing diploma on August 1, 1879, becoming the first African-American graduate nurse.

Mahoney then registered with the Nurses Directory in Boston, indicating she was available as a private-duty nurse. There were good opportunities for private nurses in those days. It took a long time to recover from an illness or operation in the late 1800s. The great advances of modern medicine, such as wonder drugs and heroic surgical operations, were still in the future. Therefore, many people were considered invalids and needed nurses in their homes. Mahoney gained a reputation as an efficient and trustworthy private nurse. She was called to work on cases as far away as North Carolina.

She was devoted to the principle that nursing is a profession, and objected to having household chores assigned to nurses. She was one of the first African-American members of the American Nurses Association, and she was an ardent supporter of the National Association of Colored Graduate Nurses (NACGN), formed by Martha Franklin in 1908. In 1909, at the age of sixty-four, Mahoney delivered the welcome address at that association's first annual convention in Boston.

Another great African-American nursing pioneer, Adah B. Thoms, was in the audience and heard Mahoney speak. In her book, *Pathfinders: A History of the Progress of Colored Graduate Nurses,* Thoms recorded her impression of Mahoney: "Miss Mahoney was small of stature, about five feet in height and weighed less than one hundred pounds. . . . She was most interesting and possessed an unusual personality and a great deal of charm. . . . She was an inspiration to the entire group of nurses present."

In 1911, Mahoney was made a lifetime member of the NACGN and appointed chaplain. As chaplain, she oversaw opening prayers and the induction of new association officers. She reportedly never missed an annual meeting.

Mahoney was also an ardent supporter of woman suffrage. U.S.

women were granted the right to vote in 1920. At the next election in Boston, held in 1921, Mahoney was one of the first women in line to cast her vote. By then she was seventy-six years old.

Two years later, she discovered that she had breast cancer. The cancer metastasized, and she died on January 4, 1926. Ten years later, the NACGN honored her by establishing the Mary Mahoney Medal to be awarded to African Americans for distinguished service to nursing. The award was continued even after the NACGN merged with the American Nurses Association in 1951.

Marie Josepha Mergler

Renowned Woman Surgeon

1851–1901

She practiced medicine for little more than twenty years. She didn't live to see her fiftieth birthday. Yet, during her brief career, Dr. Marie Josepha Mergler became one of the most renowned women doctors in the world. She was an expert at abdominal surgery; she was a medical school professor and dean; she was beloved as both a sympathetic healer and a brilliant teacher who stressed above all the moral and ethical responsibilities of a physician.

Marie Josepha Mergler was born in Bavaria on May 18, 1851, the youngest of three children in the family of Francis and Henriette Mergler. Her father was a physician who had studied at the German University of Würzburg.

In 1853, when Marie was two years old, the Merglers immigrated to the United States. The family settled in the village of Palatine, Illinois, about 20 miles (30 kilometers) northwest of Chicago. Francis Mergler established a medical practice there, and young Marie often assisted him. When she was very young she thus gained a good idea of what medicine was all about and what the life of a physician was like.

Like many young ladies of that time, Marie was educated to be a schoolteacher. She attended teacher-training colleges in Cook County and in Oswego, New York. After completing her schooling in 1872, she taught for four years at Englewood High School in Chicago.

Medicine, however, was what she really wanted, so she enrolled in the Woman's Medical College that had been established a few years before by Dr. Mary Harris Thompson. She did exceptionally well and graduated in 1879 as valedictorian of her class.

Actually landing a job as a woman doctor was more difficult. She took the test required of all seeking an appointment as physician at the Cook County Insane Asylum in Dunning, Illinois. Even though her score was the second highest, she was not even considered for the post. The authorities said an asylum was no place for a woman. Marie then went to Switzerland for a year, where she studied pathology and clinical medicine.

When she returned in 1881, she established a general medical practice in Chicago. Gradually, she became interested in obstetrics and gynecology, especially surgery in that specialty. She became the surgical assistant of a well-known Chicago gynecologist, William H. Byford, at the Woman's Hospital of Chicago. As her reputation grew, she was sought after for teaching positions. She became professor of materia medica and adjunct professor of gynecology at the Woman's Medical College of Chicago in 1882. In 1890, she became chair of the department of gynecology.

One prestigious post followed another. She was named to the staff of Cook County Hospital and Wesley Memorial Hospital. She became secretary of the faculty of Woman's Medical College (which in 1892 became Northwestern University Woman's Medical College). In 1899, she became the dean. And in 1895, she was made a professor of gynecology at the prestigious Post-Graduate Medical School of Chicago.

While teaching and practicing surgery, Marie also compiled a textbook on gynecology and helped write an article on diseases of newborns in an obstetrics textbook. Her reputation as a surgeon spread far beyond Chicago, even to Europe.

Dr. Mergler suffered from a blood disorder called pernicious anemia. This disorder occurs in people whose bodies cannot absorb vitamin B-12. As a result, not enough red blood cells are produced. In Dr. Mergler's day, pernicious anemia was fatal. She began to suffer its symptoms: weakness, loss of appetite, and finally, a damaged nervous system. Today, doctors treat pernicious anemia with injections of vitamin B-12. But no such treatment was available in 1901. That year, during a trip to Los Angeles, Dr. Mergler died of complications resulting from this blood disorder.

Sister Mary Joseph Dempsey

◆

Head of
St. Mary's Hospital,
Rochester, Minnesota

1856–1939

The young nun's introduction to nursing did not get off to a very good start. The doctor needed to undress a male patient completely in order to examine him, and Sister Mary Joseph was called upon to assist. Instead, she retreated to a corner, furious at this outrage to her modesty, and vowed she would never be put in such a position again. On later reflection, Sister Mary Joseph came to the conclusion that the suffering of sick people was of far more importance than her sense of modesty. This decision turned out to be a very good thing for the town of Rochester, Minnesota, the Mayo brothers, and the thousands of people treated by them at St. Mary's Hospital.

Sister Mary Joseph was born Julia Dempsey on May 14, 1856, in Salamanca, New York. She was one of seven children in the family of Patrick and Mary Dempsey, Roman Catholic immigrants from Ireland. Before the Civil War broke out, the Dempseys moved to a farm near Rochester, Minnesota.

The war brought another new resident to Rochester, Dr. William Worrall Mayo, who was hired as an examining surgeon for the local draft board. He liked Rochester and settled there with his wife and young son, William James, born in 1861. In 1865, another son, Charles Horace, was born. As the Mayo brothers grew older, they accompanied their father on his medical rounds, even assisting at operations on farmhouse kitchen tables. There was no doubt in anyone's mind that the Mayo boys would become doctors.

As Julia Dempsey grew older, there was no doubt in her mind that she was called to a religious life. In 1878, she took the vows of a nun in the Order of St. Francis, which the year before had established a convent and school in Rochester. Julia became Sister Mary Joseph, was trained as a teacher, and for the next twelve years taught in various schools. Her last teaching post was as director of a mission school in Ashland, Kentucky.

Meanwhile, back in Rochester, a series of events would lead Sister Mary Joseph to play a major role in the advancement of modern surgery in the United States. It began with a tornado. On a hot August evening in 1883, a thick funnel cloud descended on Rochester, sucking up everything in its path. The north part of the town was almost completely destroyed, and injured people were everywhere. Makeshift hospitals were set up in homes, hotels, even in a dance hall. Mother Alfred, head of the Franciscan convent, surveyed this situation and decided the town needed a real hospital.

Under her direction, the convent saved enough money to break ground for St. Mary's Hospital in 1887, and by 1889, the hospital was ready to open. By that time, the Mayo brothers, now called Dr. Will and Dr. Charlie, had finished medical school and joined their father in his practice. Mother Alfred persuaded the Mayos to staff the hospital, and she called back the intelligent and talented Sister Mary Joseph from her teaching post in Kentucky, to be trained as a nurse and eventually administer the hospital.

Sister Mary Joseph and the other Franciscan nuns received their training in nursing from the only graduate nurse in town, Edith Graham. Within two months, Sister Mary Joseph was the head nurse of the hospital. By 1890, she was first surgical assistant to Dr. Will. At that time, a great revolution in surgery was under way.

Before the discovery of anesthesia in the late 1840s, surgery was a horrible experience for the patient. Most operations were amputations, and the mark of a good surgeon was speed. But with the patient asleep, it was possible to perform more complex operations. Still, about half of all surgical patients died of massive infections. Then, British surgeon Joseph Lister discovered that invisible germs were responsible for infection. By killing germs in the operating room, Lister found that infections could be prevented. Now it became possible to perform surgery deep within the body, in the abdomen, head, and neck.

The Mayos made sure that the operating room at St. Mary's had the latest in antiseptic equipment—basins filled with carbolic acid to disinfect instruments and the surgeons' hands, atomizers to send clouds of carbolic acid into the air, syringes to squirt boiling water over the operating table. Operating rooms at that time were so wet that surgeons often wore rubber boots.

A cycle soon developed at St. Mary's that would turn Rochester into a medical mecca. Dr. Will and Dr. Charlie took turns traveling to the East, or even to Europe, to learn about the new operations being developed there. Then they returned to Rochester and performed tonsillec-tomies and appendectomies. They removed goiters and cancers, ulcers and gallstones. Dr. Charlie specialized in surgery of the head and neck; Dr. Will, in surgery of the abdomen.

As word of their skill spread, more patients flocked to Rochester, and by performing more surgeries, the skill of the Mayos also increased. As Dr. Will's assistant, Sister Mary Joseph also became greatly skilled in surgery. Soon, doctors were coming to learn from the Mayos. When Dr. Will would stop to explain a particular procedure to the visiting doctors, Sister Mary Joseph often went on with the operation without him. "Her surgical judgment as to the condition of the patient before, during, and after the operation was equal to that of any medical man of whom I have knowledge," said Dr. Will. "Of all the splendid surgical assistants I have had, she easily ranked first." She continued to assist him until 1915, when her administrative duties required all of her time.

Since 1892, Sister Mary Joseph had been superintendent of St. Mary's Hospital, and in that post she showed great executive ability. She had to cope with religious prejudice from some of the townspeople, rapid growth of the Mayos's surgical practice, staffing problems, and financial problems. The hospital had to support itself, separate from the Mayos, and Sister Mary Joseph watched every nickel. When a new doctor was about to throw away a piece of catgut suture, Sister Mary Joseph rapped him on the knuckles and said, "You can get three more knots out of that."

The nuns continually improved and expanded their hospital to handle the Mayos's growing practice. By 1905, the Mayos and their associates were performing four thousand operations a year. St. Mary's needed more nurses to handle this growing patient load. In 1906, Sister Mary Joseph opened the St. Mary's Hospital School for Nurses to train both nuns and laypersons. To cope with all the patients flocking to

Rochester, the Mayos brought more doctors into their practice, and the Mayo Clinic was born. In 1922, St. Mary's added a new surgical wing, and by 1930, St. Mary's, under the guidance of Sister Mary Joseph, had grown from a forty-five- to a six-hundred-bed hospital. She remained suprcrintendent of St. Mary's until her death from pneumonia at age eighty-two.

Sister Mary Joseph and the Mayo brothers all died within months of each other in 1939. Sister Mary Joseph passed away on March 29; Dr. Charlie Mayo, on May 26; and Dr. Will, on July 28. The fame of the Mayo brothers lives on in the clinic they founded; Sister Mary Joseph's name is less well-known because she shunned the limelight. Her attitude was best summed up in the remarks she made following a standing ovation at a banquet celebrating St. Mary's new surgical wing: "I do not deserve the plaudits given me tonight, but will take them and distribute them among the sisters with whom I have worked so many years trying to make St. Mary's Hospital a House of God and the Gateway of Heaven for suffering humanity."

Jane Arminda Delano

Organized the Red Cross Nursing Service

1862–1919

When war broke out in Europe in August 1914, no one expected the conflict to continue for more than a few months. Instead, it lasted until 1918, drawing in almost every country in the world. In the Great War, which would become known in history as World War I, millions of soldiers were killed or wounded, and the demands on military medical personnel were awesome. However, for the first time in history, there existed a sufficient supply of nurses to meet this great demand. The thanks for that went to the vision of an American nurse, Jane Delano, who had organized Red Cross nurses to act as reserves for the American army and navy.

Jane Arminda Delano was born on March 12, 1862, in Townsend, New York. She was the second of two daughters born to George and Mary Ann Delano. Jane never knew her father because he died during the Civil War. Her childhood was not a particularly happy one. Her mother remarried, to a widower with four daughters, and the children of the two families did not develop close ties. Then Jane's sister died in 1883, leaving her feeling especially lonely.

Like many young women of that era who had to earn their way in the world, Jane Delano seemed certain to become a teacher. After graduating from a secondary school in Montour Falls, New York, she taught at a local school for two years, until a new possibility dawned on her. One of her friends had become a nurse and gone off as a missionary to India. She, too, could take up nursing.

In 1884, Delano entered the Bellevue Hospital Training School for Nurses in New York City and graduated in 1886. A number of interesting opportunities soon came her way. First, she worked as a private nurse to the mayor of New York City, who was suffering from an attack of sciatica, inflammation of a major nerve that causes extreme pain in the leg. Then, in 1887, she served as superintendent of nurses at a Jacksonville, Florida, hospital during an epidemic of yellow fever, a viral disease transmitted by mosquitos. At her next job as nurse at a copper-mine hospital near Bisbee, Arizona, she dealt with an outbreak of typhoid fever, resulting from contaminated food or water.

In the early 1890s, she went to work at the University of Pennsylvania Hospital as an instructor and administrator. She left in 1896 to explore other career avenues and entered the University of Buffalo Medical School, but soon decided that she did not want to be a doctor. Next, she took up social work and was the superintendent of a home for wayward girls. But in 1902, she returned to the world of nursing as director of the school of nursing at Bellevue and its associated hospitals.

Jane Delano

From this position, she began the most important work of her life.

The American Red Cross underwent a reorganization in 1905, following the resignation the previous year of its founder, Clara Barton. One of the new Red Cross goals was to attract professional nurses to fill both wartime needs and needs following domestic disasters. There never had been enough trained nurses to fill the needs of military hospitals in any war. During the Civil War, for example, the nurses were hastily trained volunteers. When the Spanish-American War broke out in 1898, no plans existed for transporting trained nurses to the battlefields.

Delano became involved in the new Red Cross nurse-recruitment efforts and soon became a leader in bringing together the Red Cross and the major nurses' organization, the Nurses' Associated Alumnae (later renamed the American Nurses Association). In 1909, the National Committee on Red Cross Nursing Service was formed, and Delano was selected to chair it. That year, she also was appointed superintendent of the Army Nurse Corps, which had been established after the Spanish-American War by the efforts of a woman doctor, Anita McGee. While she held both jobs, Delano developed a plan for making the Red Cross Nursing Service the reserve for the Army Nurse Corps.

Her brilliant plan was put to the test with the outbreak of World War I. Even before the United States became involved in the war, the Red Cross sent nurses and doctors overseas. By the time the war ended in 1918, the Red Cross Nursing Service had provided some 17,900 nurses for the army and 1,000 for the navy.

Another tragedy struck in 1918. One of the worst epidemics of influenza in history swept around the world. As a result, 20 million people died, including more than 500,000 Americans. To care for the sick, the Red Cross provided more than 15,000 nurses and trained volunteers.

In January 1919, after World War I ended, Delano sailed for France to inspect the postwar facilities. There, she contracted a middle ear infection that spread to the mastoid, a part of the skull located just behind the ear. Although antibiotics are now used to treat mastoiditis, these drugs had not yet been discovered. Surgery was the only treatment available. Despite several operations, Delano was not able to recover from the infection and died on April 15, 1919.

For her outstanding contributions, she was awarded the Distinguished Service Medal of the U.S. Army and the Red Cross. She was buried in Arlington National Cemetery, and a monument was erected to her memory at the American Red Cross headquarters in Washington, D.C.

Bertha Van Hoosen

Founder of the
American Medical
Women's Association

1863–1952

Although she was one of the best gynecological surgeons in the world, the red-headed doctor's legs were trembling with fear as she prepared to do her first operation at the University of Illinois College of Medicine in Chicago. The year was 1902, and she had just been appointed the school's first woman professor of clinical gynecology. She was to operate in the school's six-hundred-seat amphitheater, a room with benches rising up in tiers so that the students could see the operating techniques being demonstrated.

She wanted her first teaching demonstration, or clinic, to go over well with the male students. But she knew it was going to be a tough day. The nurse in charge of the operating amphitheater and the two male student assistants took every opportunity to be insulting as preparations were made. After the patient was asleep, Dr. Van Hoosen went to the scrub room to wash up and put on her surgical gown. She then peeked through the amphitheater doors, but was not prepared for what she saw. There was no one there. All of the male medical students had decided to boycott the surgical clinic conducted by a woman. "My legs stiffened, my fear vanished," she wrote in her autobiography. "I was enraged! Not to give me even one chance!"

The hot-tempered, quick-witted Bertha Van Hoosen was not about to be defeated. She had selected a patient with the rarest of birth defects, an exposed bladder. The patient's internal organs literally were wrong-side out. In front of the two male assistants, Dr. Van Hoosen threw off the sheet that covered the patient. The men gasped at the sight and ran off to tell the other students. One by one, the students trickled into the room to see the rare case that the woman surgeon had brought to show them. The procession went on for three hours. Even members of the faculty came to learn about this rare deformity and the operation Dr. Van Hoosen would perform to correct it. Never again did Dr. Van Hoosen show up to find an empty amphitheater. In fact, for some of her operations there was standing room only.

Bertha Van Hoosen was born on March 26, 1863, on her family's farm in Stony Creek, Michigan. She was the youngest of two daughters born to Joshua and Sarah Ann Van Hoosen. Joshua, a man with no formal education, had been born in Canada and earned enough money digging gold in California to buy the Stony Creek farm. He then married the former owners' daughter, who was a schoolteacher.

The Van Hoosens wanted their daughters to have a college education. Bertha and her sister, Alice, attended high school in Pontiac, then studied literature at the University of Michigan. In her freshman year, Bertha made friends with two women medical students—despite the fact that her classmates shunned them and called them "hen medics." After much thought, Bertha decided that medicine was an excellent career for a woman. Her parents thought otherwise, and her father refused to pay her medical school tuition. But after earning a bachelor's degree in 1884, she enrolled in the University of Michigan's medical school and earned tuition money by teaching. She was awarded an M.D. degree in 1888.

Dr. Van Hoosen did not, however, feel she was well enough trained to treat patients. She sought more experience, first at the Woman's Hospital in Detroit, then at the State Hospital for the Insane in Kalamazoo, and finally, at the New England Hospital for Women and Children in Boston.

By 1892, Dr. Van Hoosen decided she was ready to set up a practice and, "without rhyme or reason," chose Chicago as the place after a shopping trip there with an aunt. Because there was much prejudice against women doctors, Dr. Van Hoosen at first had few patients. But with her typical resourcefulness, she sought out teaching positions to help pay the bills. She gave lectures on health for private organizations and taught anatomy and embryology at the Northwestern University Woman's Medical School.

Meanwhile, she came to realize that her first love was surgery. She continued to learn by working with the best surgeons in the city. It was an exciting time in the history of surgery. The germ theory was just coming into wide acceptance, allowing many new and wonderful operations to be safely performed. But hospital operating rooms were not all equipped for sterile surgery. After a patient almost died from infection, Dr. Van Hoosen decided to bring her own operating equipment with her. "I purchased . . . containers . . . large enough to hold gowns, sheets, sponges, etc., and a fish kettle for instruments. Everything that was to be used in the operating room I sterilized, packed, and took in the buggy with me." By then she could afford to own a buggy and a horse named Kit.

For a short time, Dr. Van Hoosen served as professor and head of gynecology at the Woman's Medical School of Northwestern University. But while reading the newspaper over breakfast one morning in March 1902, she learned that Northwestern, without warning or explanation, had closed the Woman's Medical School. For more than twenty years, no woman would again be admitted to Northwestern's medical school.

Dr. Van Hoosen was soon on the medical faculty of the University of Illinois, where she served until 1912. In 1913, she became chief of gynecology at the huge Cook County Hospital and chief of staff in obstetrics in 1920. During that time, she began to make trips every three months to the Mayo Clinic in Rochester, Minnesota, where the Mayo brothers were teaching surgeons from all over the world the latest in operating techniques. Her reputation as a surgeon grew, and in 1918, she became professor and head of obstetrics at Loyola University Medical School, the first woman to head a medical department in a coeducational school. She held this post until 1937.

Dr. Van Hoosen's main concern was with women's health issues. She pioneered in painless childbirth, using "twilight sleep," induced by injections of an anesthetic called scopolamine-morphine. She believed that women should be free of pain in childbirth, and delivered thousands of babies using twilight sleep. In 1915, she wrote a book on this subject.

Dr. Van Hoosen also was concerned with the medical education and professional advancement of women. She trained more than twenty women doctors, some of whom served as missionaries in China. As a result, she had the opportunity to visit medical facilities in China and to train Chinese women doctors in the United States.

As her fame as a surgeon grew, so did her irritation over the fact that

Bertha Van Hoosen played an important role in organizing women doctors and nurses for the U.S. armed services during World War I.

women had little professional representation. She considered American Medical Association meetings to be dreary because the few women AMA members were isolated, both socially and professionally. "A generation earlier, women doctors were on the outside standing together. Now they were on the inside sitting alone," wrote medical historian, Dr. Esther Pohl Lovejoy. Eventually, Dr. Van Hoosen came to the conclusion that women doctors needed their own organization. In 1915, she called a meeting of women doctors in Chicago, which led to the formation of the American Medical Women's Association. Dr. Van Hoosen became its first president.

Soon after, World War I broke out, and Dr. Van Hoosen appointed a War Service Committee, which established the American Women's Hospitals. These units of women doctors, nurses, and ambulance drivers served in the United States and overseas.

Dr. Van Hoosen led a long and active life. In addition to her teaching and her private practice, she enjoyed traveling abroad to meetings of the Medical Women's International Association. She usually was accompanied by her widowed sister, Alice, and her niece, Sarah, whom she treated like a daughter.

Dr. Van Hoosen suffered a stroke and died in a Michigan convalescent home on June 7, 1952, at the age of eighty-eight. She had continued to perform surgery until the age of eighty-eight.

Elsie Inglis

Heroic Surgeon
in World War I

1864–1917

Some women whose names were household words at one point in history fade from memory with the passing years. That has been the case with Dr. Elsie Inglis, a Scottish hero of World War I. She was the founder of a group called the Scottish Women's Hospitals, which sent women doctors and other women medical personnel to the battlefronts in France, Serbia, and other countries. Dr. Inglis went to Serbia, was captured, sent back to England, then returned to help Serbs fighting on the Russian front. She endured indescribable hardships of cold, hunger, and rampant disease as the Serbs retreated and were surrounded by enemy forces. She refused to leave her patients, even when her own health failed. For this dedication, she paid with her life.

Adventures in foreign lands were nothing new to Elsie Maud Inglis, who was born in India on August 16, 1864. India was then the "jewel in the crown" of the British Empire, and Elsie's father worked in the civil service there. Her father retired in 1878, and Elsie and her parents returned to Edinburgh, Scotland.

The idea of equal rights for women had started to take hold in Scotland. The outspoken Dr. Sophia Jex-Blake had succeeded in opening the medical profession to women, and Elsie Inglis decided she would like to become a doctor. Although the idea of women doctors was still widely opposed, Elsie's father wholeheartedly supported her goals. She enrolled at the Edinburgh School of Medicine for Women, which Dr. Jex-Blake had founded, and graduated in 1892. She then studied in London, Dublin, and Glasgow, and received a medical degree from the University of Edinburgh in 1899.

Inglis was appointed house surgeon at the New Hospital for Women in London, opened a maternity hospital in Edinburgh, and entered into private practice. She also went to Vienna, New York, Chicago, and even the Mayo Clinic in Rochester, Minnesota, to learn about the wonderful new operations being made possible by antiseptic surgical techniques.

In addition to becoming a skilled surgeon, she became involved in the British movement to win voting rights for women. "I have two passions in life," she said, "suffrage and surgery." The two were destined to come together in a most unusual way with the outbreak of World War I.

The British suffragettes and the British government had become bitter enemies over efforts to win the vote for women. Two powerful suffrage organizations led the fight—the National Union of Women's Suffrage Societies, which favored using constitutional means to bring about change, and the National Women's Social and Political Union, which used any means, including civil disobedience. Dr. Inglis was a leader in the Edinburgh branch of the NWSPU when the war broke out.

On June 28, 1914, a Serb assassinated Archduke Francis Ferdinand, heir to the throne of Austria-Hungary, in Sarajevo. This gave Austria-Hungary an excuse to declare war on Serbia, its long-time enemy. By August, most European countries, including Britain, were embroiled in a terrible conflict. The British suffragettes declared a truce in their war with the British government and rushed to put the thousands of women in their organizations to use in the war effort.

Dr. Inglis and other medical women offered their services to treat the wounded, but the men of the British government scoffed at the idea. In their minds it was ridiculous even to consider women surgeons in time of war. Dr. Inglis would not take no for an answer. She laid out a plan to organize the Scottish Women's Hospitals, staffed entirely by women doctors, nurses, and ambulance drivers, for service at the battlefront. "Each unit must be carefully chosen and the very best doctors must go out with them," she explained. "From the very beginning we must make it clear that our hospitals are as well equipped and as well manned as any in the field—more economical (easy!) and thoroughly efficient." She then went out lecturing and raising private funds to finance field hospitals.

Foreign governments welcomed the women's help. The Scottish Women's Hospital was invited to set up units in Belgium, France, and Serbia. At first, Dr. Inglis stayed at headquarters in Scotland, organizing the entire effort. Then, the woman doctor in charge of the Serbian unit fell ill with diphtheria, and Dr. Inglis decided to take her place.

The women doctors in Serbia had been struggling with a raging outbreak of typhus, a disease resulting from microorganisms that damage blood vessels, causing skin rashes and often fatal bleeding. Epidemic typhus is spread by the human body louse and is a common illness of wartime, thriving in the crowded, unclean conditions found among retreating armies and refugees in camps.

When the typhus epidemic was over, Dr. Inglis organized tent hospitals that could be set up just a few miles behind the front lines. The Serbs had at first driven back the invading Austrians. But soon, the Austrian army returned with Germans and other allies. Fighting fiercely, the Serbs were driven back by the enemy. The Scottish Women's Hospital retreated with the Serbian army. "We are in the very centre of the storm," Dr. Inglis wrote of the fighting, "and it just feels exactly like having the rain pouring down and the wind beating in gusts. . . ." The hospital filled with seriously wounded soldiers. British officials offered to use the British army to evacuate the women hospital staff members, but Dr. Inglis refused to leave her wounded Serbian patients. She and her staff stayed on as prisoners of the Austrian army and ran the hospital, which had up to three times as many patients as it had been designed for. Finally, in February 1916, the Austrians closed the hospital and escorted the women under armed guard to Vienna. From there they were returned to Scotland.

Rather than remain safely at home, Dr. Inglis would not rest until she could return to help the Serbian forces, which now were fighting alongside the Russians. She asked the British War Office for permission to set up a hospital unit in southern Russia. They scornfully rejected the idea. "The ordinary male disbelief in our powers cannot be argued away, it can only be worked away," she declared. Eventually, she won support from other branches of the government, and set out for the Eastern Front in October 1916.

It was not easy to reach the fighting because most routes were in enemy hands. The hospital unit had to sail to northern Russia by way of the Arctic Ocean, then travel overland through Moscow to Odessa.

The German forces overwhelmed the Serbs and Russians, and the medical women again were forced to retreat with the army. Then, the Communist Revolution overthrew the Russian government, and soon the Russian soldiers lost the will to fight. Once again, the Serbian soldiers were left without hope. Also, the Russian revolutionaries began to suspect that the hospital unit harbored spies. It definitely was time to leave. Dr. Inglis succeeded in getting permission to evacuate the Serbs who wanted to leave Russia.

By that time, Dr. Inglis was fatally ill. She had become infected with one of the microorganisms that cause dysentery, an inflammation of the large intestine that produces abdominal pain and severe diarrhea, leading to dehydration. Dr. Inglis's body already was weakened by the strain of hunger, cold, and the stress of tending to thousands of wounded soldiers.

When she arrived in Newcastle, England, Dr. Inglis mustered enough strength to walk down the gangplank and off the ship, but she died the next day, November 26, 1917. Before she passed away, family members and friends who had gathered spoke to her of the great things she had accomplished by the sacrifices she had made. With typical grace and modesty she replied, "Not I, but my unit."

Anita Newcomb McGee

Founded the
U.S. Army
Nurse Corps

1864–1940

"Remember the *Maine*" was a slogan on almost every American's lips in 1898. That February, the U.S. battleship Maine, at anchor in the harbor at Havana, Cuba, was destroyed by an explosion. Some 260 persons on board were killed, and Americans blamed Spain. At that time, Spain controlled Cuba, and relations between Spain and the United States were strained over what many Americans saw as Spanish misrule of Cuba. The Cubans were constantly rioting in protest against the Spanish.

After the *Maine* explosion, President William McKinley proclaimed Cuba an independent nation, and in April, the United States declared war against Spain. Hundreds of women, most of them untrained, deluged the government with offers to nurse sick and wounded soldiers. Dr. Anita Newcomb McGee saw this situation as an opportunity to raise the new field of trained nursing to professional status. She was an influential woman in government circles and acquired the job of screening all nursing applicants. She chose only the most qualified. After the war, she helped to found the U.S. Army Nurse Corps.

Anita Newcomb was born in Washington, D.C., on November 4, 1864, a year in which some of the bloodiest battles of the Civil War were fought. It was also a year in which volunteer nurses played important roles. Clara Barton, who eventually would found the American Red Cross, was caring for the wounded on battlefields. Dorothea Dix was overseeing the selection of nurses to care for soldiers brought to hospitals.

Anita was the oldest of three daughters in a family of intellectual individualists. Her father, after graduating from Harvard University, became an astronomer at the U.S. Naval Academy. Her mother, though not employed outside the home, was very interested in intellectual pursuits. Anita was given every educational opportunity. She attended private schools in Washington, D.C., then went abroad to study at Cambridge University in England and the University of Geneva in Switzerland.

In 1888, she married geologist and anthropologist William John McGee. Between 1889 and 1902, they had three children, one of whom died in infancy. William was a liberal, thoughtful man who expected his wife to have an independent, intellectual life outside the home. Anita McGee decided to study medicine.

She attended the medical school at what is now George Washington University, earning the M.D. degree in 1892. After taking post-graduate training in gynecology at Johns Hopkins University in Baltimore, she went into medical practice—but only for four years.

Dr. McGee's real gift was for organization. She gave up seeing patients in favor of using her organizational skills and the charm of her magnetic personality. She became a leader in the American Association for the Advancement of Science, the Women's Anthropological Society of America, and the Daughters of the American Revolution. When the Spanish-American War broke out, Dr. McGee was a well-known person in Washington, D.C. She proposed to the executive committee of the D.A.R. that the organization establish a "Hospital Corps." They agreed, and Dr. McGee became chairperson of the corps. She offered the services of the Hospital Corps to the U.S. Surgeon General. He not only accepted, but appointed her Acting Assistant Surgeon General. With volunteer help, Dr. McGee set about screening nursing applicants and eventually selected one thousand from a list of five thousand.

At first, the military doctors resisted the idea of female nurses. There had been none since the Civil War. But the nurses proved their value. Although the war lasted only from April to July and there were relatively few casualties, many soldiers in the tropical climates fell ill from yellow fever, malaria, and dysentery. One surgeon praised the nurses by saying, "When you were coming, we did not know what we would do with you. Now we do not know what we would have done without you."

For Dr. McGee, however, the success of the army nurses had political fallout. The American Red Cross, now in a period of disorganization under the controversial leadership of an aging Clara Barton, also provided nurses. Although most people agreed that the Red Cross could not have supplied all the nurses needed during the Spanish-American War, Dr. McGee's efforts generated resentment among Clara Barton supporters. They made sure that Dr. McGee, although she draft-

Dr. Anita McGee (standing, far left) with some of her nurses working in Japan in 1905

ed the legislation that created the Army Nurse Corps, never could be its head. The bill as passed by Congress stated that only a graduate nurse could be the corps' director.

Dr. McGee then organized the Society of Spanish-American War

Nurses and was its president for six years. During the Russo-Japanese War of 1904-1905, she and nine veteran nurses went to Japan and worked with Japanese nurses. She also went on an inspection tour of hospitals in Japan, Korea, and Manchuria, in China. For her efforts, the Japanese government awarded her the Imperial Order of the Sacred Crown.

Although these activities ended her active medical career, she remained interested in the nursing profession and in the Army Nurse Corps. After her death from a cerebral hemorrhage on October 5, 1940, she was buried in Arlington National Cemetery with full military honors.

Susan LaFlesche Picotte

First Native-American Woman Doctor

1865–1915

Susan LaFlesche Picotte lived all her life between two worlds: the vanishing world of the American Indian and the expanding world of white settlers in the American West. She realized that the way of white culture would replace that of her people, the native Americans. She felt compelled to serve as a bridge between both worlds. The best way to help her people, she decided, was to tend to their health, so this idealistic and determined young woman became the first Native-American woman doctor of Western medicine.

Susan LaFlesche was born on the Omaha Reservation in northeastern Nebraska on June 17, 1865. Her family was very influential in the affairs of the Omaha people. Her father even served for a time as chief. He was the son of a French father and a Native-American mother who was either Ponca or Omaha. His western name was Joseph and his Indian name, Iron Eye. Iron Eye was adopted by Chief Big Elk of the Omaha and succeeded him as chief in 1853.

Susan's mother, Mary Gale, whose Omaha name was The One Woman, was also of mixed Native-American and European parents. She and Iron Eye had five children, four daughters and a son.

Iron Eye believed that the Omaha had to learn to live as the white people lived if they were to survive. He asked his people to give up their earth lodges and tipis for wooden houses. He encouraged them to take up farming, for the great herds of buffalo had been wiped out by white hunters.

Susan and the other LaFlesche children spoke their native Omaha language while growing up on the reservation. They also learned to speak excellent English, and all the children became leaders in the Omaha community.

When Susan was old enough, her parents sent her and her sister, Marguerite, to school at the Elizabeth Institute for Young Ladies in New Jersey. Susan's oldest sister, Susette, was already a graduate of the institute and had returned to teach at the reservation school.

In 1882, after three years in New Jersey, Susan returned to the reservation and taught at a mission school. Now, as a young adult, she gained a deeper understanding of the problems confronting her people. They were having great difficulty making the switch from being a hunting people to being a farming people. They were suspicious of the U.S. government and its endless rules and regulations. Also, many Omaha were getting sick with new illnesses. We now know that the white settlers carried germs to which the Native Americans never had been exposed. Their bodies had no immunity to these germs, so they became ill and many of them died. Susan also noticed that the white doctors brought in by the government did not seem to care for the sick Indians very well. During this time, the idea of becoming a doctor took root in Susan's mind.

First she needed more education. In 1884, she and Marguerite were awarded scholarships to the Hampton Institute in Virginia. This school had been established in 1868 for the newly freed black slaves and later also accepted Native Americans. Susan was a brilliant student. She won a gold medal for scholastic achievement and ranked second in her graduating class in 1886.

While still at Hampton, she applied to the Woman's Medical College of Pennsylvania. She had no problem getting in; however, she had no money for tuition. Help came from the Women's National Indian Association, which provided aid for the professional education of Native Americans. Susan graduated first in her class of thirty-six women, earning the M.D. degree in 1889. After interning at the Woman's Hospital of Philadelphia, she returned to the Omaha reservation as Dr. LaFlesche.

Dr. LaFlesche had pledged to devote her life to helping the Omaha. She soon found out how difficult that would be. There were more than twelve hundred people living on the reservation, and she was the only doctor. When a message came that someone was sick or dying, Dr. LaFlesche had to travel to the patient on horseback or by horse and buggy, no matter what the weather. With her bags of instruments and medicines tied to the saddle, she faced bitter winter winds and deep snow drifts. In the summer, she endured the blazing sun and scorching temperatures of the Great Plains.

After four years of working twelve to fourteen hours a day, her health gave out. She began to suffer earaches and facial pains brought on by hours of travel and exposure to the biting winter cold. She no longer could carry this enormous burden alone, and was forced to resign.

The next year, she did something that surprised her friends and family—she got married. Dr. LaFlesche always had said she never would marry because she was a doctor and needed to serve her people. But she changed her mind after meeting Henry Picotte, who was half Sioux and half French. After they married in 1894, they moved to the town of Bancroft, also on the reservation. Henry farmed and Susan practiced medicine. They had two sons.

In Bancroft, Dr. Susan LaFlesche Picotte treated whites as well as Omahas. She became more than just a physician to her people. She was an interpreter and adviser and was active in church and community affairs.

Dr. Picotte's concern became increasingly focused on one particular problem: alcoholism. Unscrupulous white traders were selling alcohol to the Omaha. They even distributed samples to young children. Many adults, disheartened by the loss of traditional ways and values and discouraged about their attempts to fit into the white people's world, found escape in alcohol. Alcoholism became a severe problem among the Omaha.

Dr. Picotte struggled tirelessly against it. When she saw patients, she tried to educate them about the dangers of drinking too much. She was successful in having the sale of liquor prohibited on certain areas of the reservation, but she did not succeed in keeping the problem out of her own home. Her husband died of an alcohol-related illness in 1905.

Now a widow with two young boys, Dr. Picotte moved to the new reservation town of Walthill. Soon she was deeply involved in her new community, acting as doctor, nurse, and financial adviser. She helped organize the county medical society and headed the local board of health. She fought for the rights of her people, writing letters and visiting Washington, D.C. She even was appointed a missionary by the Presbyterian Church.

As a missionary, she set a new goal for herself: establishing a hospital on the reservation. She was able to raise ten thousand dollars from whites and Indians in the area. Under the authority of the Presbyterian Board of Home Missions, she opened the hospital at Walthill in 1913.

Dr. Picotte was head of the hospital for the rest of her life, which, unfortunately, was only two more years. She had suffered pain in her face since the days when she rode on horseback through snow and cold to call on patients. In early 1915, she had operations on her facial bones, but the surgery was not successful. She died on September 15, 1915 at the age of fifty.

Her funeral service reflected the two worlds that Dr. Picotte lived in and tried to bring together. A Presbyterian minister conducted the service, but the closing prayer was recited in the Omaha language by an elder member of the tribe.

The Dr. Susan LaFlesche Picotte Hospital in Walthill stands as a lasting reminder of her service as a doctor and leader. It was placed on the National Register of Historic Places in 1989, one hundred years after she graduated as the first Native-American woman doctor.

Annie W. Goodrich

First Dean of
Yale University
School of Nursing

1866–1954

The typical life of a student nurse at the time Annie Goodrich went into training was one of exhausting drudgery. During a twelve- to sixteen-hour day in the hospital where they were training, the student nurses would spend most of their time cleaning, scrubbing, and performing unskilled tasks. Very little time was left for lectures or learning. Goodrich quickly came to the conclusion that this was no way to train nurses. She spent the rest of her life working to raise the educational and professional standards of nursing. She headed many hospital nursing departments and even established the U.S. Army Nursing School. But her greatest dream came true when she was called upon to set up an experimental school of nursing at Yale University and to serve as its first dean.

Annie Warburton Goodrich was born on February 6, 1866, in New Brunswick, New Jersey. Her father, Samuel, was a successful life insurance representative who provided a comfortable living for his wife and their seven children. Samuel had to move several times because of his work, and he took the Goodrich family with him to New York City, London, and Hartford, Connecticut. Annie and her siblings received good educations from governesses and at private schools in London, Paris, and Connecticut. Until she reached her early twenties, Annie's life revolved around travel and social functions.

Then, the good times ended. Her mother's parents fell ill and Annie had to care for them. In addition, her father encountered financial problems, and he became ill. After her grandfather, Dr. John Butler, one of the first psychiatrists, died, Annie decided to become a nurse.

In 1890, Goodrich entered the New York Hospital School of Nursing in New York City, graduating in 1892. She discovered she had natural talents as an administrator and teacher. After graduating, she served in several administrative posts, working between 1893 and 1910 as superintendent of nurses at New York Post-Graduate Hospital, St. Luke's Hospital, New York Hospital, and Bellevue and Allied Hospitals. In all these posts, she labored to raise the educational requirements of entering student nurses, improve the nursing curriculum, and make sure the students had adequate hands-on experience in obstetrical and public health nursing.

Goodrich's reputation as a reformer grew and, in 1910, she was appointed inspector of nurses' training schools for New York State. She raised the standards of nursing education statewide, but she also came to believe that more radical reform was necessary. Nursing schools, she proclaimed, should be part of a university, where the emphasis would be placed on learning, rather than part of a hospital, where the emphasis was on providing free staff for patient care.

In 1914, Goodrich moved to an academic setting by becoming an assistant professor in the Department of Nursing and Health at Teachers College, Columbia University. In 1917, she took on the additional job of director of the Henry Street Visiting Nurse Service, which had been founded by public health nursing pioneer, Lillian D. Wald. Then World War I broke out.

The United States was faced with the problem of finding enough professional nurses to care for wounded soldiers coming in from the battlefields. The answer was the U.S. Army School of Nursing, which Goodrich organized and where she served as dean in 1918 and 1919. She set up a three-year course of study, from which the first class of five hundred nurses graduated in 1921. The school was closed in 1933 as a cost-cutting measure, but it served as a model for other nursing schools. For her war efforts, Goodrich was awarded the Distinguished Service Medal.

After the war, Goodrich returned to Columbia University and the Henry Street visiting-nurse work. Meanwhile, the Rockefeller Foundation had commissioned a study of nurses' training in the United States. The resulting report found the apprenticeship system of training nurses in hospitals inadequate and the instructors poorly prepared. The study recommended that the Rockefeller Foundation set up an experimental school of nursing to test various types of reforms in nursing education. Yale University was chosen as the site, and Annie Goodrich was chosen as the person to organize and lead the school as its first dean in 1923. Yale's nursing school at that time bestowed a bachelor's degree on grad-

Annie W. Goodrich

uates. From 1934 until the school closed in 1958, a bachelor's degree became an entrance requirement, and graduates received a master's degree.

Goodrich remained at Yale for the rest of her career. Her ideas about nursing education were very advanced. Not until the 1950s did the idea of awarding a college degree in nursing begin to take hold in other universities. Goodrich retired in 1934 to Colchester, Connecticut. She continued to lecture and consult for many years. She suffered a stroke and died on December 31, 1954.

The Golden Age of
Women Doctors

The rise of women in the ranks of Western professional medicine was related directly to the rise of the women's movement. Many jobs, formerly filled by men only, have been opened to women as a result of pressure for equal opportunities. However, the call for women physicians was one of the first demands made by feminists at the very beginning of the modern struggle for women's rights, in the mid-1800s. They regarded it as one of the most basic issues for women of that era.

The event that historians regard as marking the birth of the American women's movement was the first Women's Rights Convention, held at a Methodist church in Seneca Falls, New York, in 1848. The early leaders of the women's rights movement were the same women who had been active in the abolitionist movement to end slavery in the United States—Susan B. Anthony, Lucretia Mott, Elizabeth Cady Stanton. They came to see many parallels between the plight of black slaves and the plight of women. Women at that time had very few rights. They could not vote or own property. They were barred from schools of higher education. They were viewed by the law as being subject to the will of their husbands.

In addition, the 1800s was an age of extreme feminine modesty. Fashion dictated that women wear long, heavy dresses and lace themselves into tight corsets that literally took their breath away. Reluctance to talk about anything physical resulted in women knowing almost nothing about their own bodies or how they functioned. Sex or sexuality never was discussed in public—at least, not in the presence of women. Many women suffered silently from terrible injuries caused by difficult childbirths. If women had a gynecological problem, they were likely to keep it a secret. Untold thousands of women may have died rather than suffer the shame and indignity of being examined and treated by a male doctor. The early feminists realized that in order for women to get medical care that would free them from pain and suffering, women doctors were a necessity.

Many of the women's rights leaders in the 1800s were Quakers, members of a religious society noted for its humanitarian activities. In their demand for women doctors, the early feminists had the support of prominent male Quaker physicians.

The first to answer the call was an Englishwoman named Elizabeth Blackwell. She did not have any burning desire to become a doctor. In fact, she never had considered the possibility until a woman friend dying of a gynecological cancer begged Blackwell to study medicine. The dying woman confided that her suffering would have been less had she been treated by an understanding female doctor.

The Quaker physicians did all they could to help Blackwell get into a good medical school, but Harvard and other leading allopathic, or regular, medical schools in America would not even consider admitting a women medical student. As a joke, a small rural medical school in Geneva, New York, accepted Blackwell. She was awarded her M.D. degree in 1849—the first, and last, woman graduate from that school.

Because uniform standards for medical education did not yet exist, "irregular" schools, outside the medical mainstream, began to open their classes to women. These schools based their teachings on alternative systems of medicine, such as homeopathy, hydrotherapy, and dozens of other systems. Schools that taught what they considered the best treatments from all the competing systems were called eclectic. The

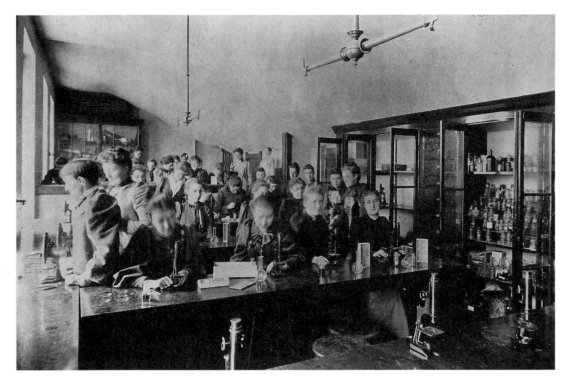

A 1903 photograph of a laboratory at the Woman's Medical College of Pennsylvania.

first American woman to earn a medical degree, Lydia Folger Fowler, graduated from Rochester Eclectic Medical School in 1850. A handful of medical schools, including Cleveland Medical College, which became the medical school of Case Western Reserve University, then admitted one or two women medical students. But the early feminists knew that a few women doctors would not be sufficient. And so they went about establishing a medical system by and for women.

The cornerstone of this system was the Female Medical College of Pennsylvania, which opened in 1850. It was later renamed the Woman's Medical College of Pennsylvania. The Philadelphia Quakers helped to launch this school. But the movement to have women doctors was gaining support from other religious leaders, such as those in the Women's

Union Missionary Society for Heathen Lands. These women objected to male doctors tending women in childbirth. "Man midwifery is unscriptural and unnatural," protested Sarah Josepha Hale, editor of *Godey's Lady's Book*. "It is an insult to the female mind and an outrage on female delicacy."

In rapid succession, regular and irregular schools devoted to educating women doctors were founded. Between 1850 and 1895, no less than nineteen women's medical schools opened. Among the regular schools were the Women's Medical College, New York Infirmary for Women and Children, established by Dr. Elizabeth Blackwell and her sister Emily; Woman's Hospital Medical College of Chicago, established in 1870; and women's medical colleges in Atlanta, Cincinnati, St. Louis, Kansas City, Missouri; and Toronto, Canada. At the same time, graduates of these women's medical schools set about establishing hospitals for women and children. By the end of the century, thousands of women doctors had been trained in women's medical schools and were practicing in women's hospitals.

The training of women doctors, which began in the United States, spread around the world. Inspired by American women doctors, an English woman named Sophia Jex-Blake undertook a long and painful struggle to open British medical schools to women. Like the women of America, the British women found that they would have to open their own medical schools and hospitals if there ever was to be a significant number of women physicians.

Then, universities in Europe began to admit women medical students: Stockholm (Sweden), in 1870; the University of Groningen (the Netherlands), in 1871; the University of Copenhagen (Denmark), in 1874; the University of Norway, in 1884. By the end of the 1800s, most Western nations were admitting women to their medical schools. Germany, which had allowed one gifted woman, Frau Dorothea

Leporin-Erxleben, to enter the University of Halle in 1754, did not open its medical schools to women until 1908.

Women doctors served on battlefields during World War I from 1914 to 1918. Women medical missionaries carried their skills and training to India, China, and the Philippines. Many women from other lands came to the United States to study at the women's medical schools.

At the same time, many state and private medical schools became coeducational. Women doctors were accepted so widely that there seemed to be no need for separate women's medical schools; one by one, they closed or merged with coeducational schools. When the 1920s began, there was only one women's medical school left—Woman's Medical College of Pennsylvania. Soon, women were once again almost entirely shut out of the medical profession.

Historians offer many possible reasons for what happened. By the late 1890s, male doctors were complaining that the field was over-crowded and that they could not make enough money. It could be that men doctors saw women as unwelcome competition. Without the balance of alternative women's medical schools, sex discrimination once again rose to the fore. Also, times were changing. Victorian ideas about a lady's modesty were becoming old-fashioned. Modern women had no qualms about being treated by male physicians.

After World War II ended in 1945, tremendous social and political forces tried to remold women into passive creatures suited only for bearing children, doing housework, and yielding to their husband's will. The arguments, though presented in scientific-sounding terms, were basically those presented in the eighteenth and nineteenth centuries: Women were not very bright, and education was not good for women. In addition, any woman who dared try to attend medical school after World War II was accused of stealing a place from a man.

It took a second women's movement to restore women to the med-

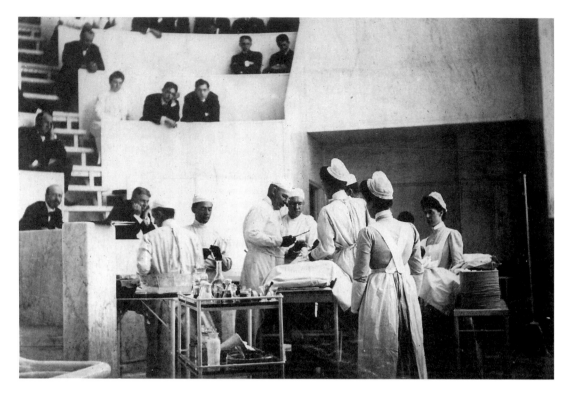

From the mid-1800s to the early 1900s, thousands of women graduated from women's medical schools in the United States.

ical profession. This time, however, the right of women to become doctors was regarded as part of a woman's right to equal educational and job opportunities. Affirmative-action programs corrected the discrimination of the past and increased the number of women in the medical profession. By the early 1990s between a third and a half of the students in medical schools were women.

Once again, women in large numbers resumed the role of healer. But the lessons of history illustrate that women should be on guard at all times. It is not impossible for the forces of discrimination to try once again to close the doors of opportunity on young women who want to be doctors.

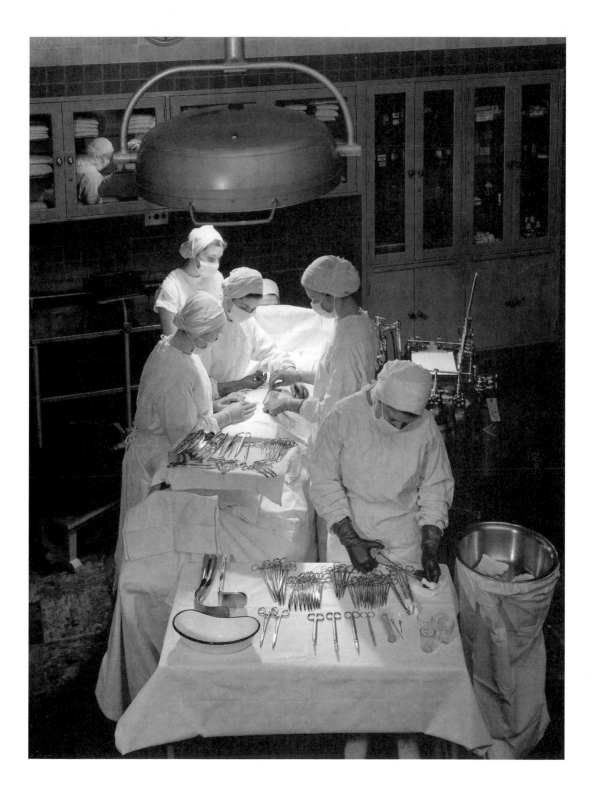

The Golden Age of Women Doctors
157

Lillian D. Wald

Founder of Public Health Nursing

1867–1940

The secure and privileged childhood of Lillian Wald in Rochester, New York, was far removed from the filthy slums of New York City's lower East Side. Yet, Lillian Wald became a nurse, left her comfortable home, and lived among the poor immigrants of New York City, trying to relieve their suffering. Because she possessed extraordinary organizational abilities as well as a tender heart, Wald made great strides on behalf of the poor. She not only helped sick individuals, she started a profession devoted to caring for and raising the health standards of millions of people—the field of public health nursing.

Lillian Wald was born on March 10, 1867, in Cincinnati, Ohio, one of four children of Max and Minnie Wald. Max Wald was a prosperous optical goods dealer. He moved his business and his family from Cincinnati to Dayton, and finally settled in Rochester, New York. There, Lillian attended a private school and at age sixteen applied to Vassar College. Vassar turned her down as being too young. Blessed with beauty and health, she turned her attention mainly to social activities, but soon felt something was missing. "My life hitherto has been—I presume—a type of modern American young womanhood," she wrote when she was twenty-one, "days devoted to society, study, and housekeeping duties. . . . This does not satisfy me now. I feel the need of serious, definite work."

The work she choose was nursing, a choice that may have been inspired by a nurse called in to care for a sister who had become ill. In 1889, at the age of twenty-two, Wald enrolled in the New York Hospital Training School for Nurses. After graduating in 1891, Wald worked as a nurse at the New York Juvenile Asylum. She soon felt the need for more education, perhaps to become a doctor. She enrolled at the Women's Medical College of the New York Infirmary for Women and Children, a school that had been founded by the first woman granted a medical degree in the United States, Dr. Elizabeth Blackwell.

While a student there, Wald was asked to set up home nursing courses for immigrant families on New York City's lower East Side. One day, she was called from class to attend a sick woman in one of the tenement slums. Wald was appalled by the horrible conditions there. The visit made such an impression on her that it changed the course of her life.

Wald decided to devote her life to nursing poor sick people. With her friend and nursing-school classmate, Mary Brewster, she moved to the top floor of a lower East Side tenement and founded the first American visiting nurse program with no ties to a religious group. She

Lillian D. Wald
160

enlisted the financial help of wealthy patrons and established what became the Henry Street Settlement, where nurses and social workers lived and worked to deliver health care and education to the residents of the community and to help with social reforms.

Wald's energetic influence extended far beyond Henry Street. She helped New York City set up the world's first public school nursing program. She lobbied for better housing, public playgrounds, special classes for mentally retarded children, and against child labor. She convinced President Theodore Roosevelt of the need for a federal Children's Bureau, which the government established in 1912.

Another great social reformer, Jane Addams, the founder of Hull House in Chicago, became Wald's friend. Together they worked as strong opponents of war. For all these causes, Wald was a tireless fundraiser. "It costs $5,000 to sit next to her at dinner," said one friend.

By the early 1930s, Wald's energy was running low. The United States was in the grip of the Great Depression. Millions of workers were unemployed, and the demands on visiting nurses and social workers were great. Her health began to fail after an operation in 1932, from which she never fully recovered. In 1933, she resigned as head worker at the Henry Street Settlement and retired to Westport, Connecticut. There, several years after suffering a cerebral hemorrhage, she died on September 1, 1940, leaving behind two books, *The House on Henry Street* (1915) and *Windows on Henry Street* (1934), and a great legacy of public health work.

Opposite page: Lillian D. Wald

Maude Elizabeth Seymour Abbott

Pioneer in the Study of Congenital Heart Defects

1869–1940

It was enough to make a strong doctor weep. Precious specimens were lying among pieces of glass from broken jars and containers. In 1907, a fire had swept through McGill University's Medical Museum, causing widespread destruction. In the smoldering aftermath, the museums' curator, Dr. Maude Abbott, got down on her hands and knees to try to rescue the organs and tissues so valuable to medical teaching and research. Dr. Abbott took her responsibility as curator very seriously. It was this kind of dedication that led her to collect a massive amount of data about congenital heart defects, a topic that was almost unknown until Dr. Abbott pursued it. Upon the foundation that she laid, future cardiologists were able to build a body of knowledge that has saved countless lives.

Maude Abbott was born in St. Andrews near Montreal, Quebec. At a very early age, she and her only sister were orphaned, and then were adopted and raised by their grandparents. Maude was an excellent student. At the age of seventeen, she entered McGill University, where she earned a B.A. degree. She then decided on a career in medicine, and applied to McGill's medical school. She was turned down because she was a woman.

But Maude Abbott was a woman with connections. The Abbotts were a prominent family in Quebec, and her cousin, Sir John Abbott, was the Prime Minister of Canada. She went to him for help. "Get the public at your back," he advised. It was advice she heeded. Public opinion almost always was in favor of her cause. In the early 1890s, however, it was too soon to sway the administration of McGill. Instead, she enrolled at Bishop's College. Its medical school was the first in Quebec to admit women students.

Nevertheless, Abbott had some rough times. A good medical education requires bedside training in a hospital. She applied to attend training clinics at Montreal General Hospital. At first, she was refused, but she went to work generating public sympathy and support. After wealthy citizens threatened to withhold their donations to the hospital, Abbott was permitted to attend the clinics. Even then, however, male students allegedly sabotaged her work to prevent her from graduating.

Despite their efforts, Dr. Abbott graduated with an M.D. degree in 1894. She then went to Europe, where all the great advances were being made, for three more years of study in medical schools and clinics. When she returned to Montreal, she worked in the wards and laboratories of the Royal Victoria Hospital.

By that time, she had developed a serious interest in heart defects.

She undertook a study of 466 cases of heart murmur, a subject about which little was known. Heart murmur is an abnormal heartbeat that can be a symptom of defective heart valves or defects between chambers of the heart. These defects may be caused by diseases, such as rheumatic fever or arteriosclerosis (hardening of the arteries). They may also result from congenital heart defects present at birth. Some murmurs may not be serious, while others could be a sign of a life-threatening problem. Dr. Abbott's paper reporting on this study was called simply "On Heart Murmurs." It was so impressive that it did much to win acceptance for women doctors in Montreal's medical society.

In 1900, Dr. Abbott was appointed curator of the McGill Medical Museum, a post she held until 1932. She also was a lecturer in pathology at McGill from 1912 to 1923, when she became assistant professor of medical research.

Meanwhile, Dr. Abbott became an international expert on congenital heart defects. McGill, which had denied her entrance to its medical school, awarded her an honorary doctor of medicine degree in 1910. The renowned Canadian physician, Sir William Osler, asked her to write the section titled "Congenital Cardiac Diseases" for his book, *System of Medicine.*

Congenital defects occur during the first weeks of a pregnancy, when the heart of the fetus begins to develop. No one as yet knows why. But most congenital heart defects are either abnormal openings or narrowed sections in the heart. Many congenital heart defects can be corrected by surgery. Dr. Helen B. Taussig developed one of the most famous of these operations, the so-called blue baby operation, for infants whose hearts are not pumping enough oxygen-containing blood.

Dr. Abbott wrote more than one hundred books and papers, including her *Atlas of Congenital Cardiac Disease,* in 1936, and *History of*

Medicine in the Province of Quebec, in 1931. In 1936, when Dr. Abbott retired from McGill, the university honored her with its highest degree, doctor of laws. She was also elected to honorary membership in the New York Academy of Medicine, the California Heart Association, and the Cardiac Society of Great Britain and Ireland.

Retirement did not mean that Dr. Abbott stopped working. She obtained a grant from the Carnegie Foundation in 1940 to write a book on heart disease. Unfortunately, she never lived to complete it. She collapsed one day while sitting for a portrait commissioned for McGill's medical building—the first one ever of a woman physician. She was rushed to the hospital, but died on September 2, 1940, of a cerebral hemorrhage.

Alice Hamilton

*Founder of
Industrial Medicine*

1869–1970

he elegant and well-bred lady must have looked out of place when she came to inspect factories and foundries. But Alice Hamilton knew more about poisonous industrial chemicals and dangerous dusts than anyone else in America. Her studies proved that lead caused illness and death among workers exposed to it in manufacturing processes. Her recommendations for making the workplace safer led to better working conditions and workmen's compensation laws for those who suffered illness or injury as a result of hazards on the job. For these accomplishments, she is known as the founder of industrial medicine.

Alice Hamilton was born on February 27, 1869, at her maternal grandmother's house in New York City. When she was six weeks old, Alice's parents took her to the Hamilton family estate in Fort Wayne, Indiana. There she grew up with three sisters, many cousins, and later, a brother, in a sheltered world of wealth and privilege. The estate had been built by her paternal grandfather, who had earned a fortune in business. The Hamilton brothers and their families lived in homes on the estate. The families had little contact with outsiders, except for members of the First Presbyterian Church. The Hamiltons were very religious and set aside Sundays for church and Bible reading.

Alice's father, Montgomery, was a partner in a wholesale grocery business, but he had no talent for this work. Instead, he loved to study languages and literature, and he passed this love along to his children. Alice's mother, Gertrude, also came from a wealthy family. She encouraged her daughters to study and to take up a career, ideas that were very radical in the late 1800s. Personal liberty, she taught them, was the most precious thing in life. Both parents encouraged the children to question everything. "We were not allowed to make a statement which could be challenged unless we were prepared to defend it," Dr. Hamilton later said. This kind of training stood her in good stead for her career as a doctor and a scientist.

Alice Hamilton received her early education at home from her parents, a teacher, and a governess. When she was seventeen years old, she was sent to Miss Porter's finishing school in Farmington, Connecticut. Attending this school was a Hamilton family tradition, but the educational standards there were not very high. There were no required courses, so Alice studied only subjects that she liked—languages, history, and literature. She avoided math and science, in which she had no interest.

This would soon change, however.

Just before Alice had left for Miss Porter's, her father's business failed, and it became clear that Alice would have to support herself. Because of the high moral ideals her family had instilled in her, she wanted above all to be useful and to make a difference in the world. She also wanted a career that would guarantee her financial independence. The one profession that would satisfy both requirements was medicine. She decided to become a doctor.

Her family was not pleased. There were still very few women doctors in the late 1800s, and Alice never had been interested in scientific subjects. She had none of the background courses she needed to be admitted to a good medical school. Undaunted, Alice took care of that problem. She first had a local schoolteacher tutor her in chemistry and physics. Then, she took courses at a third-rate local medical school. By 1892, she was ready to attend the University of Michigan's medical school, from which she graduated with an M.D. degree in 1893.

Alice became an intern at the New England Hospital for Women and Children in Boston. At this facility, Dr. Hamilton came face-to-face with the reality of poverty in America. The New England Hospital had been established by the pioneering woman doctor, Marie Zakrzewska, to train women doctors and to care for poor women and their children. While treating these patients and learning about the hardships of their lives, the social consciousness of the sheltered, privileged young Dr. Hamilton was awakened; there was no welfare system, or Medicare or Medicaid, or any other law offering protection to the working poor.

Dr. Hamilton wanted to make a difference in the lives of these people, but how to do so was not yet clear to her. She knew she did not want to be in private practice caring for individual patients. Instead, she chose to continue her studies in bacteriology and pathology. Medical scientists were just beginning to understand the importance of bacteria in causing infectious diseases, and pathologists were learning about the changes different diseases cause in the tissues and organs of the body. Dr. Hamilton pursued these subjects at the University of Michigan, then at universities in Germany, and finally at Johns Hopkins University in Baltimore. She became one of the best-trained pathologists in the world. In 1897, she was offered her first job—as professor of pathology at the Women's Medical School of Northwestern University in Chicago.

Chicago also was home to Hull House, the settlement house founded by the famous social reformer, Jane Addams. Dr. Hamilton had heard Jane Addams speak in Fort Wayne and was very impressed with her work. Hull House was located in a poverty-stricken neighborhood on Chicago's West Side. The idea of the settlement house was to have professional people live there and volunteer their services to help the poor neighborhood.

Soon after moving to Chicago, Dr. Hamilton went to live at Hull House. She set up a clinic for babies in the basement, with several tiny tubs in which Dr. Hamilton would give the neighborhood babies baths. She taught the mothers, who were mainly immigrants from Europe, the importance of keeping their babies clean. People were just beginning to understand the importance of cleanliness to good health. Some of the neighborhood mothers, fearing the cold winters of Chicago, had sewn their babies into heavy winter clothes.

Dr. Hamilton taught pathology at Northwestern until the women's and men's medical schools merged in 1902. Then, she went to work at the newly established Memorial Institute for Infectious Diseases. She investigated the cause of a typhoid epidemic in Chicago and the role of flies in spreading the germs. She even spent some time in Paris at the world-famous Pasteur Institute. All this time she continued to live and volunteer at Hull House.

At Hull House, Dr. Hamilton came face to face with many of the social and economic injustices present in the world at that time. Although she was doing all she could to help the poor, she felt she was not being very effective at making the world a better place. She saw how the families of immigrants were trapped in grinding poverty because wages were so low. She also noticed that many of the neighborhood men, who labored in steel mills, foundries, and factories, frequently became too sick to work. She concluded that their workplaces were the cause of their illnesses. She read a book entitled *Dangerous Trades,* in which the English author Sir Thomas Oliver explained that industrial workers were being poisoned by chemical dust and fumes in the workplace. Although England and Germany had set up factory inspection systems, there was absolutely no protection for American industrial workers. Company doctors kept few, if any, medical records on sick workers, and the only preventive measure was to have high turnover in the most dangerous jobs so that no one worked at them too long. Sickness and early death were considered ordinary risks of working in American industry.

Dr. Hamilton's chance to change this came in 1908, when the governor of Illinois appointed her to the new Commission on Occupational Diseases. In 1910, she became head of the state's survey of industrial poisons. Dr. Hamilton went about inspecting factories and examining workers who had taken ill. The first poison she went after was lead. Victims of lead poisoning suffered from headaches, loss of muscle control, convulsions, and even death. Dr. Hamilton identified more than seventy industrial processes that used lead and documented almost 580 cases of lead poisoning caused by these processes. By 1916, Dr. Hamilton had become the leading U.S. expert on lead poisoning and had found that serious problems can result from lead used in house paint. She also investigated the dangers of exposure to such chemicals as arsenic and cyanide. As a result of her studies, in 1911, Illinois became the first state to pass a worker's compensation law. Dr. Hamilton also negotiated with factory owners to install ventilation systems and take other steps to protect workers from dangerous substances.

Dr. Hamilton was appointed a special investigator for what became the United States Department of Labor. She worked at this task, without pay, from 1911 to 1921, inspecting factories and mines for hazardous substances. During World War I, she even inspected America's secret munitions factories.

In 1919, Dr. Hamilton was appointed assistant professor of industrial medicine at Harvard Medical School, becoming the first woman member of the faculty. She had to leave Hull House and move to the Boston area, but she continued to visit the settlement house for a few weeks every year until the death of Jane Addams in 1935. For the remainder of her career, Dr. Hamilton served as a consultant to industries wanting to improve the safety of their plants, and authored a textbook, *Industrial Poisons in the United States*.

In 1935, she retired from Harvard and took up residence with her sister at a home they owned together in Hadlyme, Connecticut. She was offered the job of director of Hull House, but turned it down. Instead, she became a consultant to the Department of Labor and spent a great deal of time testifying at hearings regarding industrial safety and investigating silicosis, a lung disease found among foundry workers, sandblasters, rock drillers, and miners, caused by inhaling silica dust. In 1938, she completed an investigation of the rayon industry, which was her last field study. She then wrote about her experiences in her 1943 autobiography, *Exploring the Dangerous Trades*.

Into her old age, Dr. Hamilton continued her long-time interest in politics and international affairs. This interest had begun just before World War I, when she joined the peace movement to prevent the great powers from going to war. From 1924 to 1930, she served on the Health

In her later years, Alice Hamilton was a nationally respected figure. This 1932 photograph shows her as the only woman member of President Herbert Hoover's committee on social trends.

Committee of the League of Nations and visited the former Soviet Union to learn about industrial health and safety there. After World War II ended, she publicly expressed her support for U.S. recognition of the People's Republic of China and, at the age of ninety-four, her opposition to American military involvement in Vietnam.

Dr. Hamilton received a great deal of recognition during her lifetime, including several honorary degrees. She died at her Hadlyme home on September 22, 1970, at the age of 101, having made a difference in the world. In 1995, the United States Post Office memorialized her life and work by issuing the Alice Hamilton fifty-five-cent stamp.

Esther Pohl Lovejoy

**Leader of
American Women's
Hospitals Overseas**

1869–1967

Esther Pohl Lovejoy became a doctor because she had a role model. In the rough, logging camp atmosphere of the Pacific Northwest, Esther encountered a woman physician, who attended her mother when Esther's youngest sister was born. The doctor made such a deep and lasting impression that Esther decided to become a doctor herself, despite the fact that her family did not have very much money. Dr. Lovejoy then went on to earn fame as a public health official, the head of the American Women's Hospitals—a major relief effort for suffering Europeans after the two World Wars—and a writer of women's medical history. Through her life and the lives of pioneering women doctors of whom she wrote, Dr. Lovejoy, in turn, provided role models for future aspiring women physicians.

Esther Pohl Lovejoy began life as Esther Clayson on November 16, 1869, in a logging camp near Seabeck in what is now the state of Washington. She was the third of six children born to Edward and Annie Clayson, both of whom had come to America from England. Edward had been a sailor in the British navy, but he jumped ship when his vessel visited the West Coast of the United States. Eventually, Edward found his way to Washington, liked it there, and sent for his wife and son in 1867. Life was hard for the Claysons. Edward tried making a living by running a hotel, selling lumber, editing a newspaper, and working a farm, but he had no success at any of these jobs.

The Clayson children did not have much opportunity for education. Esther spent a few years at a logging camp school and took private lessons in Latin and history. But when she met the woman doctor who delivered her sister, Esther reached a turning point in her life. She was determined to become a doctor.

In 1887, Annie Clayson left Edward on the farm and moved to Portland, Oregon, so that the children could find work. Esther took a job in a department store and saved her money for medical school. After a year, she had only sixty dollars; however, she won the sympathy of the dean of the University of Oregon's new medical school and was admitted as a student there in 1890. She was an outstanding student and graduated with her medical degree in 1894.

That same year, Esther married Emil Pohl, a doctor from her medical school class. They both went into private practice. He was a surgeon and she was an obstetrician. She also took time off for further study in Chicago.

Meanwhile, Esther's brothers had seen opportunities in Alaska and moved to Skagway. They set up a business selling supplies to gold prospectors bound for the Klondike. The brothers persuaded Esther and

Emil Pohl to join them and become the first doctors in the Skagway area. The Pohls lived in a log cabin, and during winter made their house calls by riding a dog sled.

All went well until 1899, when one of Esther's brothers was murdered under mysterious circumstances. Esther Pohl had had enough of Alaska and moved back to Portland. Her husband, however, stayed on, and Esther visited him during the summers. In 1901, the Pohls had a son who lived in Portland and was cared for by his grandmothers.

Esther Pohl's career flourished, and she began to take an interest in public affairs. She became a member of the Portland Board of Health in 1905, and in 1907, became its director. She was the first woman to hold such a position in a major U.S. city. She succeeded in getting regulations for improving the purity of milk, funds for school nurses, and improved sanitation standards. She also became actively involved in the fight to win the vote for women.

Tragedy loomed on the horizon, however. In 1908, her son died, apparently from drinking contaminated milk, one of the problems of great concern to her as director of the Board of Health. Then, in 1911, Emil Pohl died from encephalitis during an epidemic in the Klondike. Esther was faced with having to rebuild her personal and family life. She drew closer to her extended family, especially her nephews.

She carried on her private practice for several years, and then became involved in politics. She worked in the women's movement and actively supported the prohibition of alcohol. In 1913, Esther married George A. Lovejoy, but divorced him several years later.

With the outbreak of World War I, Dr. Esther Pohl Lovejoy addressed the need for women medical personnel on the battlefields of Europe. She tried, but failed, to convince the U.S. military to allow women doctors to serve with the armed forces. In 1917, she went to France with the American Red Cross and volunteered in a charity hospital.

In 1918, after the war ended, Dr. Lovejoy returned to the United States and gave fund-raising lectures for the newly formed American Women's Hospital (AWH), established to provide doctors and nurses to war-ravaged areas of Europe, particularly the Balkans, Turkey, and Greece. In 1919, she was made head of the AWH, a post she held for forty-eight years. Under Dr. Lovejoy's direction, the AWH established clinics, orphanages, and public health services. When the Great Depression struck in the 1930s, the AWH provided medical services for poverty-stricken areas of the United States, particularly Appalachia. After World War II, the AWH expanded its care-giving services to regions in the Far East.

Dr. Lovejoy was very active in efforts to encourage women to become doctors, increase medical jobs for women, and raise the professional standing of women physicians. She helped found the Medical Women's International Association in 1919 and was its first president. She also served as president of the American Medical Women's Association from 1932 to 1933. She recorded the accomplishments of early women doctors in several books, including *Women Physicians and Surgeons* (1939) and *Women Doctors of the World* (1957).

Dr. Lovejoy lived a long and productive life. She headed the AWH until she was ninety-seven years old. Her retirement came just five months before her death from pneumonia in New York City on August 17, 1967. But the organization to which she devoted so many years lives on as the American Women's Hospital Service of the American Medical Women's Association, providing funds, education, and health care to the poor of Bolivia, Haiti, and the United States.

Maria Montessori

---

*Famed Physician
and Educator*

1870–1952

Millions of children throughout the world have been educated at Montessori schools—or at least know some friends who attended one. The Montessori Method allows children to learn independently; teachers serve as guides for the learning process. The creator of this educational system was the brilliant Maria Montessori, the first woman to earn a medical degree in modern Italy.

Maria, the only daughter in the Montessori family, was born on August 31, 1870, in Chiaravalle, Italy. Her father was an Italian army officer who saw no need to educate girls and women. However, Maria was interested in more than household tasks. She became fascinated first by mathematics and engineering, then by biology. Her mother encouraged her and supported her efforts to win a higher education.

When Maria was twelve years old, the family moved to Rome, where she enrolled at a technical institute. She then announced her intention to study medicine, which must have caused quite an upheaval in the Montessori household. It was unthinkable for Italian women of that day to attend medical school.

With the support of her mother, Maria persisted and was admitted to the University of Rome, where she studied literature and medicine. In 1894, she became the first woman to receive a medical degree from the University of Rome.

After graduating, Dr. Montessori took a position as assistant doctor in the psychiatric clinic at the university. Many mentally retarded children were brought to the clinic, and Dr. Montessori began to do research on how to help them function better in the world. She concluded that the way in which they were taught was more important than any medical treatment they received. She found that these children learned best when they were given objects to touch, play with, and explore. With a little direction, they learned on their own.

In 1898, the Italian Minister of Education heard her lecture on this theory and was so impressed, he appointed her director of the state school for retarded children. Her work there was so successful that some of the retarded children passed national examinations in reading and writing with scores higher than those of normal children.

In 1900, Dr. Montessori returned to the University of Rome, where she studied experimental psychology and philosophy, while she lectured and served as professor of anthropology. During this time, she also taught at a women's college and worked as a practicing physician.

In 1907, Dr. Montessori had her first chance to try out her teaching method on normal children. The government put her in charge of a new school, called Casa dei Bambini (Children's House), in a dirty,

Maria Montessori doing what she loved most—helping children to learn

crowded slum in Rome. Dr. Montessori had charge of children aged
three to seven. Because she believed that small children mentally develop through the use of their senses, Dr. Montessori encouraged them to
actively touch, look, listen, smell, and taste. For example, she gave them
beads to play with in preparation for learning arithmetic. Always, her
main theme was to allow for individual initiative and self-instruction.
The work of learning, she believed, was its own reward.

Her method produced excellent results among the poor children of Rome and attracted the attention of educational officials in other countries. In 1911, the Swiss introduced her method for preschoolers. In 1917, she set up a research program in Spain. Then she went on to England, India, and the United States, lecturing and training teachers in the Montessori Method.

Dr. Montessori was made government inspector of schools in Italy in 1922, a post she held until 1934. During that time, the dictator Benito Mussolini was establishing a Fascist government. Because of the Fascist rulers, Dr. Montessori left Italy.

She went first to Spain, then to what is now Sri Lanka. Finally, she settled in the Netherlands, which she made her home for the rest of her life. Dr. Montessori wrote several books about her educational philosophy, including *The Montessori Method* (1912), *The Secret of Childhood* (1936), and *The Absorbent Mind* (1949). She died on May 6, 1952, at Noordwijk, the Netherlands, but her spirit lives on in the thousands of Montessori schools established all over the world.

S. Josephine Baker

Pioneer in Well-Baby Care

1873–1945

From 1914 to 1918, while World War I was being fought on European battlefields, Dr. S. Josephine Baker was waging a war of her own. The enemy was ignorance and disease, and the battlefield was the tenement slums of New York City. Dr. Baker was especially concerned about the thousands of babies that died each year. "It's six times safer to be a soldier in the trenches of France," she said, "than to be born a baby in the United States."

Like the Allies in World War I, Dr. Baker was victorious in her struggle. She realized that the key to saving the lives of these babies lay not in emergency treatment but in preventive care. As the first head of New York's Bureau of Child Hygiene, she organized public health education campaigns for impoverished immigrant mothers. She also helped found the federal Children's Bureau. Thanks to her efforts, the lives of thousands of babies were saved in the early 1900s, and the groundwork was laid for modern child health-care programs.

Sara Josephine Baker was born on November 15, 1873, in Poughkeepsie, New York. She was the third of four children in the family of Orlando and Jenny Baker. She preferred to be called Josephine, or just Jo, but added her first initial later in life to distinguish herself from the famous black entertainer with the same name.

Josephine's father was a successful lawyer, and her mother was one of the first graduates of Vassar College, the first U.S. women's college with resources equal to men's colleges. Jo was something of a tomboy and enjoyed a happy, carefree childhood, playing baseball and going trout fishing. As a teenager, she attended a private school. "I understood that after I left school I would go to Vassar, and then, I supposed, I would get married and raise a family, and that would be that," she wrote in her autobiography. But when she was sixteen years old, life suddenly changed. Her younger brother died, and three months later, her father died of typhoid, which he probably contracted from Poughkeepsie's contaminated water supply. Until then, the family had been quite well-to-do, but when Orlando Baker's estate was settled, a great deal of money went to pay off debts on some bad investments. As a result, little was left for the family.

Josephine felt responsible for supporting the family. She abandoned the idea of attending Vassar and announced she would become a doctor. At that time, it was not necessary to have a college degree to enter medical school. "I wish I could remember what made me choose medicine . . .," she later wrote. Almost everyone tried to talk her out of it, but, she wrote, "When I encountered only argument and disapproval, my native stubbornness made me decide to study medicine at all costs."

By then, Drs. Emily and Elizabeth Blackwell had established the Women's Medical College of the New York Infirmary for Women and Children, where Josephine enrolled. She did well in all her classes except one: "The Normal Child," a subject in which she had no interest. She failed the course and had to repeat it the following year. Determined not to fail again, she threw herself into the subject and read every book and article available. To her surprise, she found the subject fascinating and credited that experience to inspiring the work that would later save so many infant lives.

In 1898, Josephine received her M.D. degree, graduating second in her class. After serving a one-year internship at the New England Hospital for Women and Children in Boston, Dr. Baker and another woman physician rented an apartment and opened a practice in New York City. They soon learned that paying patients did not readily flock to women doctors. In her first year of practice, Dr. Baker earned only $185. The two physicians supplemented their income by doing physical examinations on women applying for life insurance policies. Then Dr. Baker saw a newspaper ad for a medical inspector at the city Department of Health. She took the civil service exam, had influential friends write letters of recommendation, and got the job. Thus began her lifelong career in public health.

Her work with babies began in earnest in the summer of 1902, when she was given the task of locating and caring for sick infants. The district for which she was responsible was called Hell's Kitchen, blocks and blocks of crowded, filthy tenements on New York City's West Side. In these buildings lived blacks and Irish immigrants. Entire families often lived in one room. During the summer, there was no ventilation, and temperatures in the crowded tenements soared. Disease bred freely under these conditions. Newborn infants were especially at risk. In the heat of summer, about fifteen hundred babies died in New York City each week. Until Dr. Baker came along, everyone accepted the fact that babies died of heat during the summer and assumed that nothing could be done about it. But the children were dying of dysentery, and the dysentery was caused by germs.

Dr. Baker came to believe that the best way to handle this problem was to prevent the disease from occurring. Over the next few years, she developed some theories about how to keep newborns healthy. In 1908, she was allowed to test her ideas. For the experiment, she selected an area with the highest rate of deaths among newborns.

The city gave her thirty school nurses—during the summer vacation—to help educate mothers of newborns about things we take for granted today: wash the babies daily, dress them in light-weight clothes rather than bundling them up in heavy blankets, take them out into the fresh air, open any windows in the apartment for better ventilation, and breast-feed the babies so that they won't get germs from contaminated milk. Dr. Baker was given a list of all the babies born every day, and she immediately sent a nurse to instruct the mother. The mothers followed the advice, and deaths among infants dropped dramatically. In the summer of 1908, there were twelve hundred fewer deaths in the experimental district than there had been the year before.

Convinced of the value of this health education, that August the Department of Health established the Bureau of Child Hygiene, with Dr. Baker as its head. She was given a staff of male doctors—who immediately resigned rather than work for a woman. She persuaded them to stay for a trial month, and after that month, they all withdrew their resignations. Many of them worked with her for years. Nevertheless, Dr. Baker always was conscious of the prejudice against women. She tried hard always to look professional and wore clothes that would allow her to blend in with the men around her. "I wore a standard costume—almost a uniform—because the last thing I wanted was to be conspicuously feminine." Her uniform consisted of tailored suits, blouses, and neck ties.

Under Dr. Baker's direction, the bureau trained and licensed midwives, placed abandoned infants with foster mothers, developed a system for preventing blindness from eye infections in newborns, distributed pamphlets containing health information, and set up Baby Health Stations where mothers could get safe milk, as well as good advice. Pasteurization, the process of heating milk to kill germs, was not yet required by law.

As the leading expert on child health, Dr. Baker was asked to lecture on this subject for the New York University Medical School, where a new degree program, Doctor of Public Health, had just been instituted. Dr. Baker agreed, but only if she could enroll as a student and work toward that degree. School officials at first said it was out of the question because the school did not admit women. The school eventually agreed to her condition because there was no one else qualified to give the lectures. She received the Doctor of Public Health degree in 1917 and lectured at N.Y.U. Medical School from 1916 to 1930.

In 1923, Dr. Baker retired from the Bureau of Child Hygiene. By that time, infant mortality in New York City had dropped from 111 to 66 for every 1,000 live births, the lowest rate for any European or American city.

Dr. Baker remained active for many more years. She served as a consultant to the U.S. Public Health Service, the New York State Department of Health, and represented the United States on the League of Nations' Health Committee. Even at the time of her death from cancer on February 22, 1945, she was serving on the New Jersey State Board of Health and the board of directors for the state reformatory for women.

Lillie Rosa Minoka-Hill

Beloved
Native-American
Physician

1876–1952

"I was sick and you visited me," reads this highest of tributes to a physician inscribed on a memorial to Dr. Lillie Rosa Minoka-Hill outside Oneida, Wisconsin. Some women doctors earned fame for scoring significant "firsts"; others, for making outstanding discoveries. Dr. Minoka-Hill earned the love of her patients in the Native-American community in rural Wisconsin by practicing her healing art with skill and compassion and serving all—regardless of their ability to pay for her service.

Lillie Rosa Minoka was born on August 30, 1876, on the St. Regis

Mohawk Indian reservation in New York State. Her mother was a Mohawk; her father, a Quaker physician from Philadelphia. When Lillie was still an infant, her mother died. Lillie's father, Joshua G. Allen, decided to leave Lillie with her mother's relatives on the reservation until she was old enough to attend school.

When she was five years old, he brought Lillie to Philadelphia, where she attended a Quaker boarding school. Dr. Allen believed it was important for Lillie to understand and appreciate her Native-American roots, so he taught her about her Mohawk heritage.

Lillie learned that the Mohawk, a tribe of Iroquois Indians, once lived near the Mohawk River in central New York. Their homes, called longhouses, were made of poles covered with bark. Mohawk men were fierce warriors and skilled hunters. Mohawk women cultivated gardens of corn, beans, and squash to supplement the nuts, berries, and plants they gathered. The Mohawk were part of an alliance of nations called the Iroquois League. Originally, the league consisted of five tribes—the Mohawk, Cayuga, Oneida, Onondaga, and Seneca. In the early 1700s, the Tuscarora also joined the league.

Lillie also learned about the Quaker half of her heritage and the Quaker principles of kindness and doing good in the world. After graduating from high school in 1895, Lillie told her father she wanted to prepare for a life of doing good by studying nursing. Her father and his family objected; they thought that studying to become a doctor was more suitable for someone with Lillie's intelligence and education. This was just the opposite of what most young women were told. Nursing was a respectable profession for young women, while medicine was not—even though women had been fighting for the right to practice medicine since the 1850s.

Lillie agreed to attend medical school. First, however, she went to a Catholic convent in Quebec to study French. She was so impressed by the nuns and their good works that she became a Catholic. Her under-standing father accepted her decision to convert.

Back in Philadelphia, she enrolled in the Woman's Medical College of Pennsylvania. She graduated in 1899 and, after interning at the Woman's Hospital in Philadelphia, she set up a private practice. She also worked at Lincoln Institute, a boarding school for Native Americans. A student there, from the Oneida tribe in Wisconsin, introduced Dr. Minoka to her brother, Charles Abram Hill.

Charles had a farm in Oneida, Wisconsin. He asked Dr. Minoka to marry him and give up her practice to become a farmer's wife. She agreed, and moved to his farm home, a primitive dwelling with no run-ning water. She combined her name with his and became known as Lillie Minoka-Hill. The couple had six children.

While tending her growing family, Dr. Minoka-Hill made friends with the medicine men and women on the Oneida Indian reservation. She learned about the roots and herbs they used as remedies. They learned that she had formal medical training. Soon, sick neighbors began coming to her for treatment with a combination of Native-American remedies and Western medicine.

Then, tragedy and hardship struck the household. In 1916, one year after the birth of their sixth child, Charles died. Dr. Minoka-Hill was left with a mortgage to pay and a family to support. Her Quaker friends asked her to return to Philadelphia, but she refused. "While in college, I resolved to spend some time and effort to help needy Indians," she replied. "In Wisconsin I found my work."

In 1917, Oneida's only licensed doctor left the town, and Dr. Minoka-Hill became the sole provider of medical care. However, she did not have a state medical license, so she could not admit patients to hos-pitals. She referred hospital cases to other doctors in the county. At what came to be known as her "kitchen clinic," Dr. Minoka-Hill saw patients at any time, from early morning to late night. She also traveled long distances to deliver babies or visit patients who were too sick to come to her kitchen clinic. She accepted only what patients could afford to pay, which ranged from a few dollars to a couple of chickens. These fees, along with a small trust fund left by her father, helped Dr. Minoka-Hill and her six children survive.

The Great Depression of the 1930s wiped out the small trust fund. Her patients, also affected by the Depression, had nothing with which to pay her. Because she did not have a license to practice, the Federal Relief Office could not reimburse Dr. Minoka-Hill for services she provided to the needy. By then, however, Dr. Minoka-Hill was renowned throughout the area for all the good that she did. Doctors in nearby Green Bay loaned her one hundred dollars to pay the application fee for the Wisconsin state medical license examination. She passed, and in 1934, obtained her first license to practice.

Dr. Minoka-Hill spent the rest of her life caring for patients in Oncida. To combat the worst problems on the reservation—malnutrition and tuberculosis—she also taught the people basic principles of nutrition, sanitation, and overall preventive medicine. She maintained her sliding-scale fees.

The local community recognized and rewarded her kindness. The Oneida tribe adopted her and gave her a name meaning "She Who Serves." The Indian Council Fire in Chicago in 1947 named her the outstanding American Indian of the year. The State Medical Society of Wisconsin gave her an honorary lifetime membership.

In the late 1940s, Dr. Minoka-Hill's health began to fail. After suffering a heart attack in 1946, she confined her practice to her kitchen clinic. A fatal heart attack ended her life on March 18, 1952, in Fond du Lac, Wisconsin.

Elsie Strang L'Esperance

Founder of Cancer Prevention Clinics

1878?–1959

*T*he Pap smear is one of the most common and successful early-detection tests for cancer. It has saved the lives of countless women who otherwise would have died of cervical cancer. The famous Pap smear was developed at a cancer clinic established by Dr. Elsie L'Esperance. Dr. L'Esperance believed in the importance of early cancer detection, and she established the first clinics designed specifically for that purpose. Her clinics served as models for the establishment of other cancer clinics throughout the United States.

Elsie Strang was was born in Yorktown, New York, probably in 1878, but the exact date of her birth has never been verified. She was the second of three daughters born to Albert and Kate Depew Strang. When Elsie Strang decided to study medicine, she was accepted at the Women's Medical College of the New York Infirmary for Women and Children in New York City. The hospital and the school for treating and training women had been established by Dr. Elizabeth Blackwell, the first woman to receive a medical degree in the United States. While a student, Elsie Strang married a lawyer, David A. L'Esperance Jr. Although the marriage did not last very long, she kept his name.

Elsie Strang L'Esperance earned her M.D. degree in 1900. She was in the last class to graduate from the Women's Medical College before it merged with Cornell University's medical school.

After serving a one-year internship at New York Babies Hospital, she went into private practice as a pediatrician, first in Detroit, then in New York City. Dr. L'Esperance became frustrated by the limited ability of medicine to cure disease in the early 1900s; she saw many sick babies that she could not help. But great findings were coming out of medical research laboratories, and she turned her energies in that direction.

In 1908, Dr. L'Esperance was appointed to the New York Tuberculosis Research Commission. Tuberculosis was a major killer at that time. Although German physician Robert Koch had proved in 1882 that a bacterium causes tuberculosis, antibiotics, which kill bacteria, had not yet been discovered. However, carefully controlled experimental techniques that would lead to such advances were being developed in medical research laboratories. One of the specialties practiced in these laboratories was pathology, the study of changes caused by disease in the cells, tissues, and organs of the body. Dr. L'Esperance became so fascinated with pathology that she took a lowly job as an assistant to a renowned pathologist, Dr. James Ewing, at Cornell University Medical

College. "It was only a technician's job," she told a New York newspaper reporter, "but I knew I could pick up a tremendous amount of information from one of the greatest pathologists in the world." His specialty was cancer.

Dr. L'Esperance had found her life's work. In 1912, she became an instructor in pathology at Cornell, and in 1920, she was appointed assistant professor. Her research focused on the pathology of malignant tumors and the search for effective treatments. At the same time, she also served as a clinical pathologist at several leading New York hospitals, including the New York Infirmary, where she was director of laboratories.

In addition to her pathology work, Dr. L'Esperance became noted for her hats, unusual concoctions of fur and feathers. This tall, slim, and fast-moving doctor often was seen wearing her hat while working in the laboratory. "There was never any place to hang the thing," she said. "So I kept it on. Got in the habit. Now I'd feel headless without it."

Two deaths in her family changed the course of Dr. L'Esperance's work in the 1930s. One was the death of her uncle, Chauncey M. Depew, a wealthy railroad executive and U.S. senator. He left Dr. L'Esperance a sizable inheritance. The other death was that of her mother—from cancer. By then, Dr. L'Esperance had become convinced that cancer could be treated effectively if it was diagnosed early enough. She and her sister used their inheritance to found, in their mother's honor, the Kate Depew Strang Tumor Clinic at the New York Infirmary. They thought that setting up cancer clinics in their mother's name "made more sense than a stained-glass window."

The first clinic for diagnosing and treating cancer in women opened in 1933 under the direction of Dr. L'Esperance. In 1937, she opened the Kate Depew Strang Cancer Prevention Clinic, devoted to the early detection of cancer in women. This clinic was staffed entirely by women physicians. Another Strang Cancer Prevention Clinic was opened at Memorial Hospital for Cancer and Allied Diseases and expanded its focus from women to include men and children. The founders of other cancer prevention clinics around the country looked to the Strang Clinics as their model.

Research also was conducted at the Strang clinics. Researchers there discovered that proctoscopic exams revealed cancers of the colon and rectum before there were any symptoms. But perhaps the most famous discovery was the test for cervical cancer developed by Strang researcher George Papanicolaou. The Pap smear is now performed on millions of women every year.

In 1942, Dr. L'Esperance returned to Cornell's medical school as assistant professor of preventive medicine. In 1950, she became a full professor, the first woman to hold that academic rank at Cornell, and retired that same year.

Even in her retirement, Dr. L'Esperance remained active. She was a member of several medical societies and hospital boards, and served as a consultant to the New York Infirmary until 1955. She always had been active in women's medical associations. She was president of the Women's Medical Society of New York State from 1935 to 1936, and of the American Medical Women's Association from 1948 to 1949. In addition, she was the editor of two women's medical journals.

Dr. L'Esperance died at the home she shared with her sister in Pelham Manor, New York, where she loved to raise horses, on January 21, 1959.

Margaret Sanger

Founder of the
American Birth
Control Movement

1879–1966

The visiting nurse had been called to a New York City tenement where a young Russian woman was lying in a coma. Within minutes, the young woman died. The cause of her death was her attempt to abort a baby. Her three children huddled in a corner, wailing, and her husband began sobbing and pulling his hair. It was a scene that nurse Margaret Sanger never would forget. Only three months before, she and a doctor had been called to this same apartment and the young woman had begged the doctor for information on how to prevent pregnancy. The young couple were living in poverty and could not afford to have any more children, and an abortion would surely kill the mother. However, it was illegal then to give out information on contraception, so the doctor suggested that the husband sleep on the roof.

This tragic experience, and the fact that thousands of women were trapped in poverty from bearing so many children, moved Margaret Sanger to action. She learned all she could about birth control. She wrote books and articles, opened clinics, and even went to prison because she broke the law forbidding the distribution of such information. In the end, she succeeded in changing the laws, and founded what became the Planned Parenthood Federation of America. But the controversy over reproductive rights is one that continues to this day, involving complex moral and religious, as well as social and medical, issues.

Margaret Sanger was born Margaret Louise Higgins on September 14, 1879, in the factory town of Corning, New York. Her mother, Anne, and father, Michael, had eleven children. Margaret's mother was a devout Roman Catholic; her father, a free-thinking atheist. Margaret's parents loved and respected one another, and she loved both of her parents dearly. Her father, a maker of stone monuments, encouraged his children to be independent thinkers and to challenge authority.

Margaret's first act of rebellion was against her eighth grade teacher, who made cruel remarks about a new pair of gloves, a gift from Margaret's older sister. Margaret refused to return to that school, so her sisters scraped up enough money to send her to a private school. After three years of study, she took a teaching job in New Jersey. She soon found that she did not like teaching, and so she was not reluctant to return home when word came that her mother was very ill with tuberculosis.

Anne Higgins died at the age of forty-nine. Margaret blamed her mother's death on exhaustion from years of childrearing as much as from tuberculosis. Michael Higgins wanted Margaret to move back home and be his housekeeper, but they had a serious quarrel, and Margaret left home to become a nurse.

She entered a nursing school in White Plains, New York. To complete her course of study, the school sent her for practical training to a New York City hospital. There, she was introduced to a young architect and artist, William Sanger. The couple fell in love and were married in 1902. They settled down in a New York suburb and, by 1910, had three children.

Eventually, the Sangers grew restless and dissatisfied with their suburban lives. They saw many injustices in the world and wanted to do something to help. New and radical ideas were stirring in arts and politics. Wanting to be part of the new movement, the Sangers moved to New York City and joined the Socialist Party. Margaret helped organize strikes by workers in Massachusetts, Pennsylvania, and New Jersey. To earn money, she worked as a home nurse, caring for sick people and women giving birth in their homes. She met and was influenced by the great radical leaders of the day, including labor leader William Haywood and feminist Emma Goldman. She became convinced that poor women never would be able to improve their lives until they could control their bodies.

She began to learn all that she could about birth control. First, she read all the material available in New York libraries. Then, she and her husband went to France, where she gathered information on how the French practiced contraception. Armed with this information, she returned to the United States and began publishing information about sexuality in her new magazine, *The Woman Rebel,* which first appeared in March 1914. After several issues, the U.S. government charged her with violating the federal law forbidding the distribution of birth control information. She learned she could be sentenced to forty-five years in prison, and so she left for Europe again. Before she sailed, she left instructions to have her pamphlet, *Family Limitation,* distributed. This pamphlet contained the most detailed information on birth control then available in English.

Margaret spent a year in Europe, and discovered that there were birth control information centers in Holland, staffed by midwives. She also met and became friends with English psychologist Havelock Ellis, a pioneer in studies on sexuality. Ellis convinced Sanger that she should abandon her militant feminism and instead, try to convert the middle class to her views about birth control.

While Margaret was in Europe, Bill Sanger was arrested and sent to prison for distributing *Family Limitation.* She decided it was time to go home and face trial. A few days after her return in October 1915, her daughter died of pneumonia. By then, the actions of Margaret Sanger were making front page news. Her husband's imprisonment and her daughter's death turned public sympathy in her favor. The government dropped the charges.

Margaret Sanger then decided to establish a birth control clinic. She and her sister opened the Brownsville Clinic in Brooklyn, New York, in October 1916. Ten days after it opened, the police shut the clinic down. Sanger and her sister were arrested, tried, and sent to prison. But an appeals court judge ruled that, while it was illegal for the sisters to distribute birth control advice, it was not illegal for doctors to do so. Even though she went to jail, Margaret Sanger believed she had won a great victory.

At that point, her struggle for legal birth control began a new phase. She campaigned for birth control clinics staffed by doctors and lobbied to have the laws changed. Wealthy socialites and philanthropists contributed money to her cause. During this time, Margaret Sanger moved away from her radical past. In 1921, she founded the American Birth Control League, which became Planned Parenthood Federation of America in 1942. She divorced Bill in 1920 and in 1922, married a millionaire, J. Noah Slee, who helped to fund the birth control cause.

In 1923, Sanger opened the first birth control clinic in the United States to be staffed by doctors, the Birth Control Clinical Research Bureau in New York City. Under the direction of a woman physician, the bureau did the first real research on the effectiveness of birth control methods. Doctors could also go there to learn about birth control techniques. In 1936, a federal court ruled that birth control information was not obscene and thus not illegal. By 1938, there was a network of more than three hundred birth control clinics around the United States, most of them staffed by women physicians. One of the greatest victories came in 1937, when the American Medical Association ruled that giving out advice on contraception was a proper service for a doctor to perform.

Margaret Sanger's ideas gained new respect with the baby boom that occurred after World War II. In 1952, she helped found the International Planned Parenthood Federation and served as its first president. She longed to find a birth control measure that was controlled entirely by the woman, a vision that finally became reality when she learned that a biologist, Gregory Pincus, had developed a birth control pill. She brought his work to the attention of those who could bring it to market, and the first birth control pill was sold in 1960.

Six years later, on September 6, 1966, Margaret Sanger died of heart failure in a Tucson, Arizona, nursing home. During her lifetime, she had seen the issue of birth control move from being considered obscene to being considered a legitimate medical matter. She never believed, however, that the victory was permanent. "I am often asked," she wrote, "'Aren't you happy now that the struggle is over?' But I cannot agree that it is. Though many disputed barriers have been leaped, you can never sit back, smugly content, believing that victory is forever yours; there is always the threat of its being snatched from you. All freedom must be safeguarded and held."

Elizabeth Kenny

Developed Treatment for Polio

1880–1952

I n the lonely expanses of Australia's frontier, or outback, a child fell ill with a disease that the young nurse, Elizabeth Kenny, had never seen before. In the outback, where there were few doctors or nurses, most of the medical care was delivered by "bush nurses" like Elizabeth Kenny, resourceful women with a little medical training and a lot of courage and heart.

Bush nurse Kenny decided she had better get help. She sent a telegram to the nearest doctor, 40 miles (60 km) away in the town of Toowoomba. The symptoms, she explained, began with a sore throat and stiff neck; then the child's limbs became paralyzed and wracked with painful muscle spasms. The doctor telegraphed back that it sound-ed like infantile paralysis, or polio. He had no suggestions about what Kenny should do. "Use your best observation and judgment," the message said.

Not knowing that the standard treatment for polio was to keep the paralyzed armas and legs immobile, Kenny first wrapped the child's limbs in hot cloths, then massaged and manipulated them. Eventually, the child recovered with no crippling after effects. This was the first case of polio treated by Elizabeth Kenny, but certainly not the last. Her treatment, developed in the Australian outback, would save thousands of children around the world from the crippling effects of polio and make her name a household word in the days before polio vaccines.

Elizabeth Kenny was born near Warialda, New South Wales, on September 20, 1880. Her parents were immigrants from Ireland and Scotland. She was their fifth child. When Elizabeth was eleven years old, the family moved to an isolated farm near Nobby, Queensland. As a young woman, she decided to become a nurse and serve the people in the Australian outback. In 1907, she began her training at a hospital in Sydney. When her training was completed, she opened a tiny hospital in an isolated settlement, where she encountered her first few cases of polio.

World War I broke out and in 1915, Kenny enlisted in the Australian Army Nursing Service. Her job was to care for wounded soldiers being brought back to Australia on transport ships. Some of the soldiers had suffered wounds that left their legs paralyzed. She spent hours moving the paralyzed limbs for them, a system called passive exercise. She made fifteen round-trips on the ships, and became absorbed in how to care for paralyzing injuries. During this time, she invented a special stretcher for supporting and transporting wounded soldiers. She began to be called "Sister," the title for head nurses in the British medical system.

After the war ended, Sister Kenny went back to being a private nurse in the outback. She would have spent the rest of her life serving the medical needs of the Australian frontier had a polio epidemic not struck Queensland in 1933.

At that time, polio was an illness that terrified people all over the world. It most frequently struck children, and there was no way to prevent it and no way to cure it. Medical scientists now know that polio is caused by a virus that attacks nerves in the brain and spinal cord. Fearful parents would watch their children for signs of a polio attack. Some polio attacks are mild; others, severe. In severe cases, the child's neck and back would become stiff and the muscles weak. They would suffer pain in their back and legs. If the attack was severe enough, they could become paralyzed temporarily. Some polio patients with paralyzed chest muscles required the mechanical assistance of an "iron lung" in order to to breathe.

Although there have been vaccines against polio since the late 1950s and polio cases are now rare, there still is no cure. The best treatment is based on the techniques of Sister Kenny: complete bed rest; hot, moist bandages to relieve pain; and passive exercise of the patient's limbs to prevent crippling deformities.

In 1933, Sister Kenny set up a clinic in Townsville, New South Wales, and treated polio patients with her method. As news of her success spread, other clinics were set up in Queensland. Not everyone was enthusiastic about Sister Kenny's work, however; conservative doctors called her a charlatan. They said the limbs should be immobilized in splints from four to eight weeks to prevent the weakened muscles from straining the healthy ones. These doctors feared that her methods would cripple some polio patients. To settle the matter, in 1935 Sister Kenny and the conservative doctors agreed to have a government committee study her work. Influential conservative doctors served on this

Sister Elizabeth Kenny (right) adjusts the cap worn by actress Rosalind Russell. Russell was portraying Kenny in a 1945 biographical movie called Sister Kenny.

Elizabeth Kenny
202

committee, however, and the final report condemned the Kenny method.

Sister Kenny continued to believe that she was doing the right thing for polio patients. She had seen so many recover completely. She decided to take her case before the people of the world. She used the press and politicians to help win public support. She went to other countries to demonstrate her polio treatment, receiving her warmest welcome when she arrived in the United States in 1940. The University of Minnesota and the National Foundation for Infantile Paralysis supported her work and found that her methods were sound. The American Medical Association gave Sister Kenny its approval, and she raised public support and funds to establish the Elizabeth Kenny Institute in Minneapolis for treating polio patients and training care-givers in the Kenny method.

Although she treated thousands of polio patients, Sister Kenny never charged them a cent. She lived a very simple life, supported by royalties she earned on the stretcher she invented during World War I.

Sister Kenny was so beloved in the United States that Congress passed a measure allowing her to come and go as she pleased without a visa. A 1951 opinion poll showed that she was the woman most esteemed by the American public. A motion picture was made about her life, and she was encouraged to become a U.S. citizen.

Sister Kenny preferred to remain an Australian. When she became very ill, she returned to Toowoomba in the Australian outback, where she died on November 30, 1952. By that time, the Kenny method had become widely accepted in her homeland. Though she had received many honorary degrees and other awards for her work, perhaps the most touching tribute was the custom of schoolchildren in Queensland beginning their day with a prayer asking a special blessing on Sister Kenny and her work with the polio patients.

Elizabeth Kenny

Gladys Rowena Dick

Discovered Cause of Scarlet Fever

1881–1963

*C*hildhood was a dangerous time before antibiotics came into use in the 1950s. Parents were always on the alert for the sore throat and bright red skin rash that signaled the onset of scarlet fever in a child. Scarlet fever was a widespread and serious illness that sometimes proved fatal. Children who survived the scarlet fever infection often developed serious complications, such as rheumatic fever or kidney disease, later in life. No one knew what caused scarlet fever until Gladys Rowena Dick and the doctor she married discovered that a bacterium was responsible. They went on to develop the first ways to prevent and treat this dread disease.

Gladys Rowena Henry was born on December 18, 1881, in Pawnee City, Nebraska, where her father had settled after a career as a cavalry officer during the Civil War. She was the youngest of three children, and soon after she was born the family moved to Lincoln, where there were better schools.

As a young girl, Gladys loved biology. She attended the University of Nebraska and earned a B.S. degree in 1900. She announced that she would like to attend medical school, but her mother opposed this idea. Instead, Gladys taught high school biology and took graduate classes in zoology at the university. She never gave up her desire to study medicine, however, and finally her mother gave in. Gladys Henry was accepted into Johns Hopkins School of Medicine in Baltimore in 1903. In 1907, she received her M.D. degree. Soon after, she had the opportunity to work in medical research, doing studies on experimental heart surgery and blood chemistry.

Meanwhile, her mother had moved to Chicago. In 1911, Dr. Henry obtained a position at the University of Chicago and moved there to be close to her mother. At the University of Chicago, she made two acquaintances that would alter the course of her life: scarlet fever research and Dr. George Frederick Dick.

Gladys and George were married in 1914. They went off on an extended and romantic honeymoon to Egypt and the Balkans, just before World War I broke out. After returning to the United States, they established their home in Evanston, a suburb north of Chicago, were Dr. Gladys Dick set up a private medical practice and also served as pathologist at Evanston Hospital. George and Gladys became members of the John R. McCormick Memorial Institute for Infectious Diseases. The institute had been founded by the McCormick family after a son died of scarlet fever.

The husband and wife team began working together to solve the mystery of scarlet fever. They suspected that a microorganism called streptococcus was the cause of the disease. It took them ten years to prove it. The experiment they performed could not be done today, because research practices and medical ethics have changed. But in 1923, people could volunteer to be the subjects of dangerous tests. So the Dicks injected two volunteers with a strain of streptococcus and, sure enough, the volunteers became ill. Streptococcus was the culprit. This bacterium is also responsible for strep throat and a number of other infections, including impetigo and blood poisoning. Scarlet fever can follow any of these infections.

Next, the Dicks discovered that the bacteria produce a toxin, or poison, which causes the scarlet fever rash. Using this knowledge, they were able to develop a skin test to identify people who would be likely to develop scarlet fever if infected with streptococci. They also tried using the bacteria to immunize people against infection, and they developed a substance called an antitoxin to treat scarlet fever. Antitoxin is usually made by injecting a toxin into an animal. The animal's immune system produces an antitoxin in the animal's blood serum. The serum is then used as a drug to counteract the toxin.

In the early 1920s, to make sure that the preparations would always be of high quality, the Dicks applied for patents on their immunization process and treatments with antitoxin. Patents for medical treatments are not unusual today, but in the 1920s, the Dicks were strongly criticized on the grounds that patents would interfere with research. The Dicks protested that they did not apply for the patents for financial gain.

Their scarlet fever research won the Dicks many honorary degrees and prestigious awards. Yet, controversy over the patent issue continued for years, until a development that made it meaningless—the introduction of penicillin and other antibiotics. Today, strep throat and other strep infections can easily be cured with antibiotics, and scarlet fever is no longer the threat it once was.

In the later years of her career, Dr. Gladys Dick turned her attention to another dreaded disease, polio. She also pursued her longtime interest in child welfare. She had helped found the first professional adoption organization in the United States, the Cradle Society in Evanston. When she was forty-nine years old, she and her husband adopted two babies, a boy and a girl.

In 1953, Dr. Gladys Dick retired, and she and George moved to Palo Alto, California. She died in California on August 21, 1963.

Florence A. Blanchfield

Superintendent of U.S. Army Nurse Corps During World War II

1884–1971

Japanese war planes swooped down on Pearl Harbor, home of the U.S. Navy's Pacific Fleet, on the morning of December 7, 1941, and World War II began for the people of the United States. The terrible toll of Americans killed or wounded also began and would not end until 1945. Playing a major role in seeing to it that thousands of wounded soldiers were cared for and evacuated from the battlefields was a small, sandy-haired nurse of amazing calm and efficiency—Colonel Florence Blanchfield.

Florence Blanchfield was born on April 1, 1884, in Shepherdstown, West Virginia. When she was growing up, the world of work outside the home was just beginning to open up for women; the field of professional nursing had been established only twenty-four years before she was born.

It took young Florence some time to discover what she wanted to do with her life. After completing her secondary education, Blanchfield headed for Pittsburgh and the Martin Business College, where she took a secretarial course. Not content with a secretarial career and feeling the need for more education, she took courses at the University of California and Columbia University in New York City. Finally, she enrolled at the South Side Training School for Nurses in Pittsburgh, graduating as a nurse in 1906.

Blanchfield had become particularly interested in surgery. She signed up for post-graduate training at an institution called Dr. Howard Kelly's Sanitorium and at Johns Hopkins Hospital, where she studied surgical technique and how to supervise operating rooms. From then until 1917, she worked as an operating room supervisor and overall nursing supervisor at hospitals in Pennsylvania and as an industrial nurse at the United States Steel plant in Bessemer, Pennsylvania. In 1913, she spent a year as a nurse in the Canal Zone of Panama. She finally found her true calling as an army nurse when the United States entered World War I in 1917.

After joining the Army Nurse Corps in August 1917, she sailed for France in September. The war in Europe had been raging since August 1914 between the Central Powers (led by Austria-Hungary and Germany) and the Allies (led by France, Britain, and Russia). Some of the worst fighting occurred along what was called the Western Front, which extended across Belgium and France to the Swiss border. There, both sides had dug huge systems of trenches. Each side alternated shelling and infantry attacks against the other side's trenches. Neither side could make any progress, and the Western Front remained deadlocked in trench warfare until 1918.

Thousands of soldiers were killed or wounded as they fought over the space between opposing trenches, called no man's land, which varied from about 30 yards (30 m) to a mile (1.6 km) wide. There was a constant stream of casualties flowing from the front lines to the hospitals in the rear. Most of the wounds were from bombs or shrapnel, but some of the worst injuries were caused by poison gas. Blanchfield and the other army nurses tended the wounded at military hospitals and at auxiliary hospitals set up in homes, churches, and schools.

World War I ended in 1918, but Blanchfield stayed on in France until May 1919. After returning to the United States, she left active military service for a few months. Then, in early 1920, she rejoined the Army Nurse Corps, and stayed there for the remainder of her professional career.

The 1920s and 1930s were peaceful years for the U.S. military. Blanchfield served at several base camps in the United States and in the Philippines, rising to become a chief camp nurse and serving for a brief time as an instructor at the Army School of Nursing. She even spent a year in China. In 1935, she was assigned to duty in the office of the U.S. surgeon general.

After the bombing of Pearl Harbor, America became embroiled in the most terrible war the world had ever seen. Blanchfield was made a lieutenant colonel, and in 1942, became first assistant to the superintendent of the Army Nurse Corps, Colonel Julia Flikke. Soon after, Colonel Flikke became ill and retired. Blanchfield took her place as head of the army nurses and was granted the relative rank of full colonel. Nurses at that time were given "relative" military rank rather than full army commissions.

Colonel Blanchfield assessed the battlefield needs and called for an additional two thousand new army nurses for each month of 1943. She insisted that the nurse recruits be trained in military customs, physical endurance, and working under battlefield conditions. She made sure they could do their wartime jobs. "They are hardened, I assure you." Colonel Blanchfield told a reporter at the time.

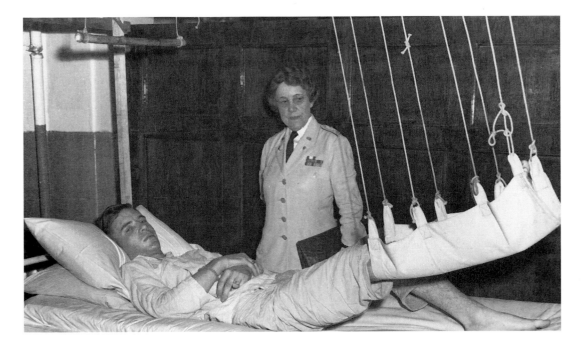

Colonel Florence Blanchfield visits with an American soldier who was injured in World War II.

World War II had a profound effect on the way nurses were regarded in U.S. society. For the first time, the federal government recognized nurses as a professional group and appropriated millions of dollars for nursing education. Thousands of nurses worked in hospitals overseas and in the United States tending the sick and wounded soldiers.

World War II ended in 1945, and Colonel Blanchfield retired from the Army in 1947 as the first woman to receive a regular army commission as an officer. She continued to be active in such organizations as the American Nurses Association, the National League of Nursing Education, and the Retired Officers Association. She died on May 12, 1971.

Karen Danielsen Horney

*Pioneering
Psychiatrist*

1885–1952

Childhood was not a particularly happy time for Karen Danielsen Horney. She resented her authoritarian father and felt that both her parents loved her brother best. Although she was very beautiful, she began to think of herself as ugly. If she could not be beautiful in her own eyes, she decided, she would be smart, and eventually she became a doctor. Then, her own inner conflicts drew her toward the new field of psychoanalysis.

After going through analysis and becoming an analyst herself, Dr.

Horney began to question some of the basic ideas that Sigmund Freud, the founder of psychoanalysis, had put forth regarding women. Dr. Horney was the first Freudian to disagree with Freud's ideas about women's emotional issues. She developed her own theories about female psychology and about emotional disorders of both men and women. These theories became very important to psychologists and psychiatrists, and today influence how they treat people with emotional problems.

Karen Danielsen was born on September 16, 1885, in a village near Hamburg, Germany. Her father, Berndt, was a Norwegian sea captain who became a German citizen and worked for the Hamburg-American Lines. He held authoritarian religious beliefs, felt that the husband should be the head of the household, and that women should be meek and obedient. Karen's mother, Clotilde, was Dutch, and more cultured and educated than Karen's father. She was more liberal in her religious views and believed in more independence for women.

From the time she was quite young, Karen had conflicting feelings about her father. She hated his gruff, authoritarian ways, but she also wanted his approval. She believed that her mother and father were more fond of her older brother, and she felt rejected and unwanted. She was very intelligent, however, and determined to be a success in life. When she announced that she intended to become a doctor, Berndt was against the idea. Karen's mother helped change his mind, and Karen went off to study medicine at several German universities, earning an M.D. degree in 1911 from the University of Berlin.

Meanwhile, in 1909, she met and married an economics and political science student, Oskar Horney. Between then and 1915, they had three daughters, and Dr. Horney was faced with the problems of raising a family and fulfilling residencies in her chosen specialties—neurology and psychiatry. Life events began to close in on her. Her mother died.

Conflicting feelings again rose up regarding her father. She felt torn between her duties to her family and her career. She began to feel tired and depressed, so she sought help through the new technique of psychoanalysis in which the patient "free-associates"—talks freely about memories, thoughts, and dreams while the analyst interprets them.

Dr. Horney disagreed with some details, but believed in the basic ideas of psychoanalysis and became trained as an analyst herself, taking her first patients in 1919. From 1920 to 1932, she taught at the Berlin Institute for Psychoanalysis. Then, she was offered the post of assistant director of the Chicago Institute for Psychoanalysis. By that time, she had separated from her husband, whom she divorced in 1937. Dr. Horney and two of her daughters moved to the United States. She became a naturalized U.S. citizen in 1938.

After two years in Chicago, Dr. Horney went to New York City to teach at the New School for Social Research and the New York Psychoanalytic Institute. She also set up a private practice. By then, her disagreements with Freud were becoming greater.

She had long been interested in issues regarding female psychology. As a trained scientist, she observed that Freud's theories often did not fit her patients. She published her own theories in two books in the 1930s, *The Neurotic Personality of Our Time* and *New Ways in Psychoanalysis,* in which she openly disagreed with several of Freud's basic ideas.

The split between Dr. Horney and the Freudians widened until, in 1941, the New York Psychoanalytic Institute disqualified her. Immediately, she and several like-minded colleagues established the Association for the Advancement of Psychoanalysis and a teaching branch called the American Institute for Psychoanalysis, of which Dr. Horney was made dean. She also established and became editor of the *American Journal of Psychoanalysis.*

Dr. Horney's own ideas about psychotherapy began to develop further. She came to believe that all people naturally seek self-realization, a deep understanding of their inner being. Anything that interferes with this natural tendency, she believed, created emotional disorders, which at that time were called neuroses.

Until the end of her life, Dr. Horney was busy lecturing, seeing patients, writing books, and furthering her own understanding. In November 1952, she became ill. The diagnosis was advanced cancer of the bile ducts. Her condition rapidly grew worse, and she died less than a month later on December 4, 1952.

Over time, Dr, Horney's ideas have gained increasing influence. Her theories are built into most methods of psychotherapy practiced today.

Anna Freud

Pioneering Child Psychoanalyst

1895–1982

After the Nazis came to power in Germany and then took over Austria during the 1930s, many famous Jewish intellectuals fled to foreign countries to escape persecution and death in concentration camps. Among them was the family of Anna Freud. Her father, Dr. Sigmund Freud, was one of the greatest thinkers of all time. His theories regarding the human mind formed the basis for modern psychiatry. He taught his technique of psychoanalysis to his daughter, and she became the main guardian of psychoanalytic theory after her father died. Anna Freud also made her own major contributions to psychiatry and psychology, especially in the area of child development.

Anna Freud was born in Vienna, Austria, on December 3, 1895. She was the youngest of six children in the family of Sigmund and Martha Freud. After completing her formal education, she became an elementary school teacher. In 1937, she founded the Jackson Nursery in Vienna. Meanwhile, she was being trained in the psychoanalytic methods developed by her father.

Sigmund Freud had developed a complex theory of how the human mind works. His psychoanalytic theory dealt with behavior, the components of the mind, and how to treat mental disorders.

His recommended treatment, psychoanalysis, consisted of having the patient free-associate; that is, talk about anything that came to mind. Freud would then analyze these free associations, along with the patient's dreams, in an effort resolve the patient's inner conflict.

Freud also believed that all psychoanalysts should go through analysis themselves. As part of her training, Freud psychoanalyzed Anna.

In 1938, the Freud family fled to London, where Anna Freud continued her psychoanalytic practice. The next year, two events occurred that greatly affected Anna Freud's life. Her father died of cancer, and Britain became engaged in World War II. Anna Freud now was responsible for carrying on her father's work, which always had been controversial, and which now faced competition from other theories. Then, in 1940, Germany began full-scale air raids on London, an attack known as "The Blitz." Although The Blitz ended in 1941, German air raids on London continued until the war ended in 1945. A total of some thirty thousand Londoners were killed, many of them leaving behind orphaned children. Anna Freud set about helping these war orphans.

In 1940, she helped to establish and became director of the

Anna Freud

Hampstead Nurseries in London, a home for children whose parents had been killed or otherwise separated from their families. Anna Freud and a colleague, Dorothy Burlingham, closely observed the children and prepared monthly reports on their progress and behavior. Freud not only helped the children; her studies helped lay a foundation for theories about child development and about how children react to danger, fear, and loss. She concluded that it was separation from parents, not the terrors of war, that was most destructive to the children.

After the war, the Hampstead Nurseries became the Hampstead Child Therapy Course and Clinic. Here, Anna Freud psychoanalyzed children, conducted research on child development, and helped train other child analysts. She also helped edit her father's papers.

Anna Freud's interest in child development led her to consider custody issues that result in children being separated from their parents. In the 1960s, she carried out studies at Yale University in New Haven, Connecticut, on child custody laws and how they affect children. She and two Yale professors wrote two books in the 1970s, *Beyond the Best Interests of the Child* and *Before the Best Interests of the Child*. They argued that removing a child from its natural parents is more psychologically damaging to the child than the abuse or neglect they might suffer at the hands of that parent. This argument has had a major impact on how social workers and courts handle foster care and adoption cases.

Anna Freud continued to direct the Hampstead Clinic and lecture on children's rights until the time of her death on October 8, 1982. She also served as vice president of the International Psycholanalytic Association from 1938 to 1982. Although she never received either an M.D. or a Ph.D. degree, honorary doctorates were bestowed on her by such prestigious institutions as the University of Chicago and Columbia, Harvard, Yale, and Vienna universities. Her work changed society's view of the best way to bring up children, from one in which stern discipline was the primary tool for assuring healthy development to one in which guidance and gentle restraint have become the norm.

Helen B. Taussig

---

*Co-Developer
of "Blue-Baby"
Operation*

1898–1986

Dr. Taussig watched anxiously as the surgeon operated on the heart of a six-year-old boy, a so-called "blue baby," whose skin had a bluish tinge from a lack of oxygen. The child was so weakened by the lack of oxygen in his blood that he could no longer walk. Helen Taussig had developed a theory of what caused blue babies and had helped to devise a way to cure them. Now, surgeon Alfred Blalock had just finished carrying out her ideas on the heart of this boy. It was the third such operation the team had done in 1944. Even before the surgery was over, the boy's skin color was changing from blue to pink. "I walked around to the head of the table and saw his normal, pink lips," she said. "From that moment, the child was healthy, happy, and active."

Although she is best known for her work on blue babies, Dr. Taussig made many important contributions to the understanding of heart abnormalities in children. She also played a major role in determining that the tranquilizer, thalidomide, was causing birth deformities in Europe, and alerted U.S. authorities to this danger.

Helen Brooke Taussig was born into a family of scholars on May 24, 1898, in Cambridge, Massachusetts. Her mother, Edith, who died when Helen was eleven, was one of the first women to graduate from Radcliffe College. Her father, Frank, was a well-known economist and professor at Harvard University. Her grandfather had been a highly respected specialist in eye diseases of children.

With this family background, there was no question that young Helen would pursue a higher education. First, she attended the Cambridge School for Girls. Then, like her mother, Helen enrolled at Radcliffe. She grew to be a tall, blue-eyed athletic young woman and became a Radcliffe tennis champion. After two years, she transferred to the University of California at Berkeley, where she earned a bachelor's degree in 1921.

On the long, hot, dusty train ride from California to Massachusetts, Taussig thought about her future. A career in medicine appealed to her, but when she discussed it with her father, he thought the public health field would be better suited to a woman. Harvard was going to open a school of public health in the autumn of 1922, and Frank Taussig urged his daughter to apply. Harvard's medical school would not accept women, but Professor Taussig assumed that the school of public health would be open to women. He was wrong. Women would be allowed to take courses, but they never would be awarded a degree.

This kind of prejudice only made Helen Taussig more determined to study medicine. She began by taking a course on histology (tissue studies) at Harvard. "I was allowed to attend lectures, but I sat up in the far corner of the room by myself," she recalled. "And when I looked over the [microscope] slides, I was in a separate room and not allowed to speak to any of the men." She could take courses on bacteriology and immunology, but not anatomy. For anatomy, she had to go to Boston University.

One day, the anatomy professor at Boston University handed her a beef heart and told her, "It won't do you any harm to get interested in one of the larger organs of the body as you go through medical school." And that is how Helen Taussig's life-long study of the heart began.

The same professor advised her to apply to Johns Hopkins Medical School, one of the few open to women. In the late 1800s and early 1900s, there had been many women's medical colleges, but these closed after a number of regular medical schools opened to women. Soon, however, the co-educational schools began to limit the number of women who could attend, or closed their doors to women completely. Johns Hopkins originally had been funded with money from a group of women who insisted that this medical school always admit women equally with men. Taussig was admitted to Johns Hopkins Medical School and graduated with an M.D. degree in 1927.

Johns Hopkins Hospital was less generous toward women. Dr. Taussig had wanted to intern there in the specialty of internal medicine. But they would allow only one woman intern in that specialty—and they already had one. Dr. Taussig had to settle for pediatrics, which turned out to be very fortunate for thousands of infants not yet born.

Dr. Taussig had been interested in the functioning of the heart since the day the beef heart had been thrust into her hands. After completing her internship in 1930, she was appointed head of the children's heart clinic at the Harriet Lane Home, the pediatric division of Johns Hopkins, where she remained for her entire career.

Soon after Dr. Taussig began her work at the heart clinic, new equipment became available. She was given the additional assignment of studying congenital heart defects with X rays, an electrocardiogram machine, and the fluoroscope that had recently been delivered. A fluoroscope uses X rays, but allows a physician to view internal body organs—such as a beating heart—while they are actually functioning. Dr. Taussig used the new equipment to study the heart of every young patient that came to the clinic. She kept careful records of what she observed during physical exams and related them to what she saw on the medical images.

One day, a blue baby was brought to her. The outlook for these children was not good. Usually, they became increasingly ill until they died of "heart failure." Dr. Taussig examined the child and concluded there was a defect in the heart. As she studied more blue babies, she theorized that, because of heart defects, their blood was not getting sufficient oxygen from the lungs.

Normally, bluish-colored blood containing the waste gas carbon dioxide returns from the body to the right side of the heart and is then sent to the lungs. The lungs remove the carbon dioxide and replace it with oxygen. The red, oxygen-containing blood flows to the left side of the heart, ready to be pumped throughout the body. But heart defects in a blue baby, Dr. Taussig reasoned, prevent the blood from gathering enough oxygen from the lungs. She determined that the heart abnormalities in blue babies included defective heart valves, holes between the chambers of the heart, and heart chambers too small to pump blood properly. But the most important defect was a narrowing or blockage in the pulmonary artery, the blood vessel that connects the heart to the lungs.

Until 1938, no one had repaired a human heart, but that year an American surgeon closed an abnormal opening in an artery in the heart of a child. This gave Dr. Taussig a grand idea: if blood flow in an artery could be closed off, why couldn't blood flow also be opened up? If the blockage in the artery of a blue baby could be bypassed, normal blood flow could get to the lungs and pick up life-giving oxygen. Not until 1941 did she find a surgeon willing to develop this type of operation. That year, Dr. Alfred Blalock arrived at Johns Hopkins and was willing to work with Dr. Taussig on an operation to help correct the abnormal blood circulation in blue babies.

Dr. Blalock thought he could take one of the arteries leading to the arm and use it to carry blood around the blocked heart artery. For almost two years, he tested operating techniques on dogs in his laboratory. Finally, in 1944, Dr. Taussig and Dr. Blalock decided to try out the operation on three blue babies. What became known as the Blalock-Taussig operation worked wonders, and over the years saved the lives of thousands of babies.

In 1946, Dr. Taussig was appointed associate professor of pediatrics at Johns Hopkins and in 1959, became the first woman to be made a full professor at the school. Meanwhile, she carried out other important studies on congenital defects and recorded her findings in a book, *Congenital Malformations of the Heart,* published in 1947. She also trained many pediatricians and kept in touch with them over the years.

In 1962, one of her former students, who had become a pediatrician in West Germany, paid her a visit. He told her that many children in Germany and Great Britain were being born without limbs. He suspected that a new sleeping pill might be the cause. This so disturbed Dr. Taussig that she immediately made plans to go to Europe and investigate these birth defects for herself. In Europe, she talked to doctors and examined patients and medical records. She concluded that a drug called thalidomide, taken as a sedative by pregnant women, was to blame. She returned to the United States and warned that this drug never should be approved for use in America. She also urged the U.S.

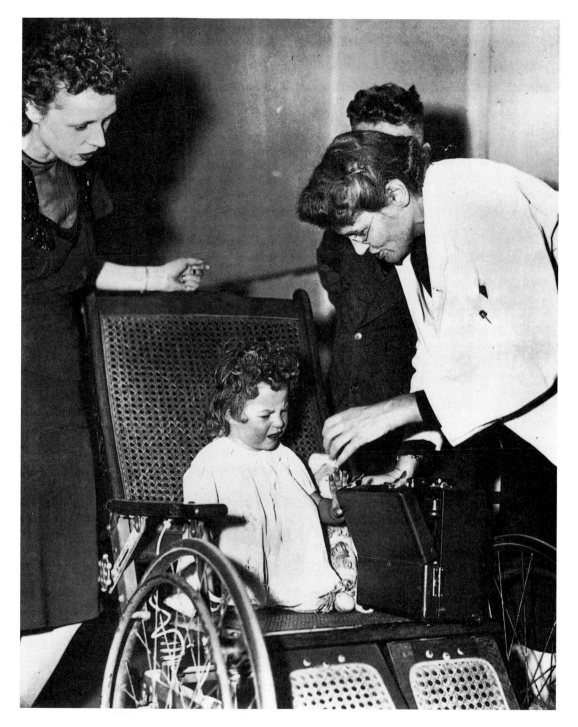

Dr. Helen Taussig (right) examines a child with a heart condition in 1945.

government to be more careful in its drug testing. As a result, she helped prevent many tragedies.

In 1963, Dr. Taussig retired from Johns Hopkins, but she continued to do research on congenital heart problems. She spent her summers on Cape Cod, as she had since childhood, and the rest of the year at her home in a suburb of Baltimore, Maryland. She served as an alternate delegate to the World Health Organization and as a delegate to the International Red Cross. Dr. Taussig's life ended suddenly when she was killed in an automobile accident on May 20, 1986, four days short of her eighty-eighth birthday.

During her lifetime, Helen Taussig was a leading woman doctor, and honors were showered upon her. In 1947, the French government made her a chevalier of the Legion of Honor. She was given the prestigious Albert Lasker Award in 1954 and honorary degrees from many universities, including Harvard and Boston universities. In 1964, she was given the highest civil award by the president of the United States, the Medal of Freedom. The next year, she was elected the first woman president of the American Heart Association.

A newspaper reporter once asked Dr. Taussig what motivated her work in the service of humanity. "Everybody enjoys feeling he can contribute," she replied. "It is the greatest feeling in the world—whether one contributes to the family, community, or country."

Hattie Elizabeth Alexander

Pioneer in the Diagnosis and Treatment of Meningitis

1901–1968

Whenever an infant or young child was brought to the hospital in convulsions, the young medical intern braced for the worst. She would ask the parents how long the child had been ill and what the symptoms were. If the child had been ill less than 24 hours, had run a fever, was vomiting, and then became extremely sleepy, Dr. Hattie Alexander suspected that the cause was bacterial meningitis. Before 1940, this disease was almost certainly fatal, killing within a matter of hours. The sight of children being stricken with this disease made a deep impression on the young intern. She decided to devote her medical career to developing a treatment for it, and she succeeded.

Hattie Elizabeth Alexander was born on April 5, 1901, in Baltimore, Maryland. Her father was a local merchant; Hattie, her mother, and seven brothers and sisters lived in a house in downtown Baltimore. She attended a high school for girls and was awarded a partial scholarship to Goucher College.

In college, she loved sports and spent more time in athletic activities than in academic ones. She was barely a C student. As a young person, Hattie Alexander loved fun, and she remained a fun-loving person all her life. In later years, she especially loved to race around in her speedboat.

While in college, however, she developed a serious interest in the new and growing field of bacteriology, the study of microscopic organisms, some of which cause disease. After graduating from Goucher in 1923, she was hired as a bacteriologist, first by the United States Public Health Service, then by the Maryland Public Health Service. During that time, she decided she would attend medical school. After working for three years years, she saved enough money to enter Johns Hopkins School of Medicine.

As a medical student, she was brilliant. She received her M.D. degree in 1930, and served two internships in pediatrics, one at the Harriet Lane Home—Johns Hopkins' hospital for children—and the other at Babies Hospital of the Columbia-Presbyterian Medical Center in New York City. It was at the Harriet Lane Home that she saw her first heart-breaking cases of meningitis.

Meningitis is an infection most commonly caused by bacteria or viruses. The infection attacks membranes, called the meninges, that cover the brain and spinal cord.

Although several types of bacteria can cause meningitis, Dr. Alexander focused her attention on one particular species of bacteria— *Haemophilus influenzae*. (Despite its name, *Haemophilus influenzae* has nothing to do with the flu.)

Dr. Alexander carried out her research while she was working as a staff pediatrician and clinical instructor at Columbia's medical school. She began as an instructor in pediatrics in 1935 and rose through the ranks to become a full professor in 1958. She also was in charge of the Babies Hospital laboratory, where tests on patients were analyzed and research carried out. Although she was fun-loving in her personal life, she was all business in the hospital. She had a great ability to organize her time and to concentrate on the task in front of her. This discipline allowed her to treat patients, teach students, and conduct laboratory research.

Working with immunochemist Michael Heidelberger, Dr. Alexander prepared the first effective treatment for bacterial meningitis. It was a substance called an antiserum. Dr. Alexander had followed closely the work of other medical researchers experimenting with substances from the blood serum of infected animals. Serum, the clear liquid part of blood, contains antibodies, molecules produced by the body's immune system to attack specific germs. Antiserum is made by injecting an animal with a bacterium, then collecting the blood serum, which now has antibodies to that bacterium.

Dr. Alexander made an antiserum to *Haemophilus influenzae* by injecting rabbits with large amounts of bacteria. She then injected the antiserum this produced into patients suffering from meningitis. In 1939, she reported the first cure of this otherwise fatal infection. She did not stop there. In her search for ever more effective treatments, she experimented with other drugs in the 1940s, the sulfa drugs and the early antibiotics. Thanks to the work of Dr. Alexander and researchers who came after her, bacterial meningitis usually can be cured in a few weeks with doses of antibiotics.

In her work with bacteria, however, Dr. Alexander was one of the first to recognize a problem that has grown more serious in the 1990s—

bacterial drug resistance. In laboratory cultures, she observed that, over time, a strain of bacteria could not be killed by a drug that once was able to kill it. She correctly concluded that this was due to genetic mutations (changes in the genes). When a batch of bacteria are exposed to an antibiotic, almost all of them die off. But a few remain because they have genes with mutations that make them resistant to the drug. Over time, these resistant bugs multiply until they become the main disease-causing strain. Dr. Alexander was one of the first doctors to study the genetics of bacteria.

In 1965, Dr. Alexander served as the first woman president of the American Pediatric Society. She became professor emeritus in 1966. She received many other awards and honors for her work. Then cancer struck, and Dr. Alexander died on June 24, 1968.

Women in Medical Research

Not all women doctors are involved in treating patients. Some devote their careers to medical research, seeking answers to questions about health and disease in laboratories around the world and even as doctor-astronauts in space.

Women medical researchers have made many important discoveries. Some of them have won Nobel Prizes for their work. Many of them rose to the top of their profession despite widespread prejudice against

Gerty Cori and her husband, Carl Ferdinand Cori

women doctors and researchers.

The first woman doctor to win a Nobel Prize for physiology or medicine was Gerty Radnitz Cori. She shared the 1947 award with her husband, Carl, for their work on how the body stores sugar and other carbohydrates.

Gerty Radnitz was born in 1896 in Prague, the capital of what is now the Czech Republic. While attending medical school in Prague, she met Carl Cori. They married and, in the 1920s, immigrated to the United States. It was almost impossible at that time for women to find jobs in medical research. During one interview,

Rita Levi-Montalcini

Gerty Cori was told it was "un-American" for a woman to work in research with her husband. After working at a cancer research center in New York, she and her husband were offered jobs at Washington University in St. Louis, Missouri. There, they refined their understanding of the carbohydrate cycle and the way in which sugars and starches are used or stored in cells, and the role that insulin plays in this process.

An Italian woman doctor, Rita Levi-Montalcini, won a Nobel Prize in 1986 for her research on how nerves grow and develop. Dr. Levi-Montalcini, born in Turin in 1909, came from a Jewish family of intellectuals. To become a medical researcher, she first had to overcome her father's opposition to the education of women, and then the anti-Semitic terrors of the Italian fascists during World War II. After the government of Italian dictator Benito Mussolini passed laws forbidding Jews to practice medicine, Dr. Levi-Montalcini set up a research laboratory in her bedroom. She made tiny instruments out of sewing needles and conducted research on the development of nerve cells in chicken embryos. After the war, she published a paper on her findings and, as a result, was invited to do research at Washington University in St. Louis. While there, she discovered an important biochemical substance called nerve growth factor, which won her the Nobel Prize. She also worked in Italy as the director of a major research laboratory in Rome.

Women researchers other than trained doctors also have made major contributions to medical science. Women biologists and chemists, for example, have added greatly to our knowledge about genes, the basic blueprint of cells and cell functions. Genes are responsible for all inherited characteristics. In the early 1900s, American biologist Nettie Stevens discovered that a person's sex is determined by chromosomes, tiny structures in the cell that carry the genes. She found that a female has two X chromosomes; a male has one X and one Y chromosome.

One of the major advances in biological science was the discovery in the 1950s of the structure of DNA, the molecule of which genes are made. A key factor in this discovery was a set of sophisticated pictures of DNA made by aiming X-ray beams at DNA samples. The pictures were made by a British molecular biologist and X-ray crystallographer named Rosalind Franklin. Her images showed that the molecule was shaped like a twisted ladder. Without her consent or knowledge, biologists James Watson and Francis Crick used her pictures to create the now famous model of the DNA molecule. They shared in a 1962 Nobel Prize for this work. Rosalind Franklin had died of cancer in 1958. So whether she would have been included in the Nobel Prize had she lived will remain forever unknown.

Barbara McClintock

A woman biologist who did win a Nobel Prize for her genetic studies was Barbara McClintock. In the early days of genetic research, scientists conducted studies either on fruit flies or on corn. McClintock worked with corn. She discovered strange patterns in the corn kernels she was breeding and in the early 1950s, concluded that this could only result from genes changing places on the chromosome. At the time, genetic scientists believed that genes were strung along chromosomes like beads on a string, and so it was impossible for them to jump around. It took about twenty years for these genetic scientists to catch up to McClintock. Her theory of transposable elements, or jumping

Gertrude Belle Elion

genes, was proved correct. Jumping genes play a major role in genetic engineering and may be responsible for some cancers caused by genetic mutations (changes).

Biochemist Gertrude Belle Elion earned a Nobel Prize in Physiology or Medicine in 1988 for her role in developing some of the most revolutionary drugs of this century, including treatments for leukemia, gout, herpes infections, and AIDS. She also helped develop a drug that made organ transplants possible. After years of being turned down for graduate school fellowships simply because she was a woman, Elion went to work in 1944 at the Burroughs Wellcome Research Laboratory in Tuckahoe, New York. She was assigned as laboratory assistant to George Hitchings, who was trying to make new drugs by synthesizing chemicals similar to ones that occur in nature. Using this technique, during her career Elion made one breakthrough drug after another. The Nobel Prize was only one of many honors bestowed on Elion during her brilliant career.

Many important discoveries in pediatric medicine were made by women researchers. Dr. Virginia Apgar developed a widely used system

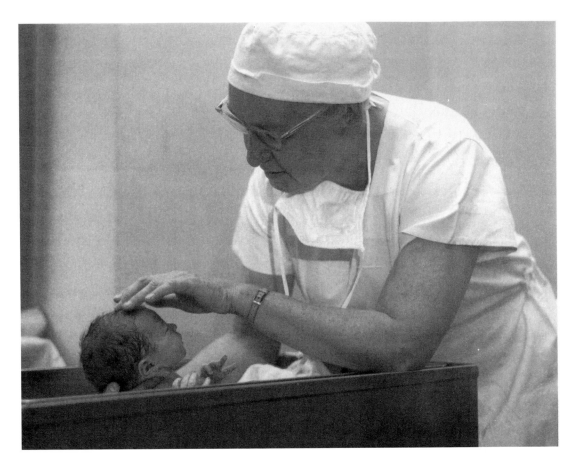

Dr. Virginia Apgar examines a newborn baby.

for evaluating the health of newborns. After graduating from medical school in 1933, Dr. Apgar set out to specialize in surgery. Two years later, she switched to the growing field of anesthesiology. She was especially interested in anesthesia during childbirth. After years of observing newborn infants, she developed what became known as the Apgar Score, a system for evaluating the health of the newborn based on heart rate, breathing, muscle tone, reflexes, and color. The Apgar Score is used to determine whether an infant needs special medical treatment during the first few hours of its life.

Other women doctors who made great contributions to pediatric medicine include Dr. Helen Taussig, who devised an operation for so-called blue babies, infants whose hearts are not pumping enough oxygen in- to the blood. Canadian cardiologist Maude Abbott also made major contributions to the understanding of congenital heart defects in children.

One of the best-known women medical researchers during the first half of the twentieth century was Dr. Florence Sabin. Her statue stands in the U.S. Capitol in Washington,

Dr. Florence Sabin

D.C. Dr. Sabin, born in Colorado in 1871, actually had two distinct medical careers. Her first career was devoted to important studies of blood cells, the lymphatic system, and how the body's immune system fights tuberculosis. By the time she retired in 1938, she had earned many honors and awards for this research. But instead of retiring quietly with her sister in Denver, she became interested in public health matters. As head of a state committee on public health, she determined that Colorado's public health system was corrupt and inefficient. She devised the Sabin Program to control infectious disease, ensure the purity of milk sold to consumers, and provide for the adequate treatment of sewage. She became one of the most beloved figures in Colorado and in 1951, at the age of eighty, she was honored with the Lasker Award, the most prestigious award in medicine.

With the dawn of the Space Age, women doctors went into orbit to conduct research. America's first female African-American astronaut was physician Mae C. Jemison. After graduating from Cornell Medical College in 1981, Dr. Jemison served as a

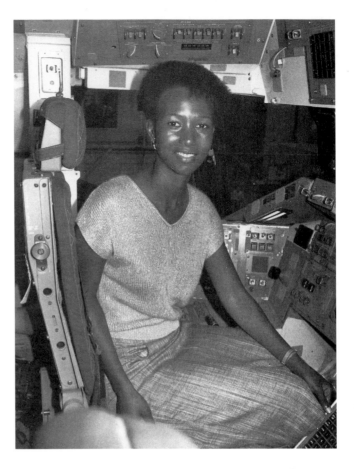

Mae Jemison is both an astronaut and a doctor.

Peace Corps medical officer in West Africa and then worked as a physician with a health maintenance organization in Los Angeles. All the while, she dreamed of becoming an astronaut. She was accepted into astronaut training in 1987 and qualified as a mission specialist in 1988. Dr. Jemison's first space flight was aboard the space shuttle *Endeavor*. While in orbit, she conducted experiments to test the effects of weightlessness on a range of animals—from flies and frogs to human beings.

Although individual women have made important contributions to medical research, almost all major medical studies—especially on heart disease and cancers—have been designed by men and conducted by men on male volunteers. As a result, a great deal is known about how diet, exercise, and such factors as smoking affect the health of men. Very little is known about how such factors affect the overall health of women. Cardiologist Bernadine Healy is one person working to remedy this situation. Dr. Healy served as the first woman director of the National Institutes of Health from 1991 to 1993. In this important administrative position she established the Women's Health Initiative, a fifteen-year study of various factors that affect women's health. With women taking on such administrative responsibilities, future medical research projects may provide great benefits to the health of women.

Dorothy Hansine Andersen

Recognized Cystic Fibrosis as a Disease

1901–1963

She was not what the medical establishment considered ladylike. Her hair was always in disarray, her clothing a mess, and she was covered with ashes from the cigarette that seemed always to be dangling from the corner of her mouth. Worse, she loved to ski, hike, and go canoeing. But worst of all, in the eyes of her more conservative colleagues, was the fact that her hobby was carpentry. She bought a farm in northwest New Jersey and with her own hands built a fireplace and chimney, put on a new roof, and made most of the furniture. Dorothy Hansine Andersen didn't really care what the medical establishment thought. She followed her own instincts both outside and inside the hospital and laboratory. Those instincts led her to discover cystic fibrosis as a distinct disease and to find a simple test to diagnose it.

Dorothy Hansine Andersen was born on May 15, 1901, in Asheville, North Carolina, the only child of Hans Peter and Mary Louise Andersen. Adolescence was difficult for Dorothy. When she was thirteen years old, her father died. Her mother suffered from poor health, and Dorothy had to assume responsibility for her care. In 1920, her mother died, and Dorothy was left without any close relatives.

She did, however, have the money to pursue an education. She attended Mount Holyoke College, and graduated in 1922. She then enrolled in Johns Hopkins Medical School and did research in the laboratory of the famous anatomist Florence Sabin. In 1926, Dr. Andersen earned her medical degree and then served an internship in surgery at Strong Memorial Hospital in Rochester, New York. Simply because she was a woman, the hospital would not allow her to pursue further training as a resident in surgery or join the staff as a pathologist. She had to look for a position elsewhere.

The pathology department at Columbia University's College of Physicians and Surgeons took her on as an assistant. In 1930, she became an instructor in pathology at the medical school, while she continued post-graduate studies. In 1935, she became an assistant pathologist at Babies Hospital of the Columbia-Presbyterian Medical Center, and there began the work for which she became renowned.

One of Dr. Andersen's tasks was to perform autopsies. One December day in 1935, while doing an autopsy on a young child, she noticed an abnormality in the pancreas. She decided to look into this further. She searched out all the hospital records that related to similar problems and analyzed them. A clear pattern of disease emerged. Dr. Andersen had identified a previously unrecognized disease, and she called it cystic fibrosis.

The first signs of cystic fibrosis appear in infants or young children. Their bodies produce abnormally thick mucus, which causes blockages and infections in such organs as the lungs, pancreas, and liver. At the time Dr. Andersen identified the disease, cystic fibrosis inevitably resulted in death from a blockage in the intestines or a severe lung infection.

After identifying the disease, Dr. Andersen set about looking for a diagnostic test. The first test she developed involved a complicated analysis of protein in fluid taken from the duodenum, the first part of the small intestine. She and her research team then discovered that children with cystic fibrosis have abnormally high levels of salt in their perspiration. This discovery led to a simpler test, which doctors still use to diagnose cystic fibrosis.

Meanwhile, Dr. Andersen slowly progressed up the career ladder. In 1945, she was appointed assistant attending pediatrician at Babies Hospital and in 1952, was named chief of pathology. In 1958, she became a full professor at Columbia's College of Physicians and Surgeons.

In addition to her cystic fibrosis discoveries, Dr. Andersen made an important contribution to the development of open-heart surgery. Early in her career, she began to collect hearts of babies who had died of congenital heart defects before or after birth. In the 1940s, surgeons began to experiment with heart surgery, but they knew little about the hearts of embryos or infants. They came to Dr. Andersen for help and advice. She developed a training program in congenital heart defects that soon became a requirement for heart surgeons wanting to operate at Babies Hospital.

At the same time, Dr. Andersen was exploring issues involving cystic fibrosis. She experimented with drug treatments and studied the disease in patients who survived to young adulthood. She also explored the genetic basis of this inherited disease.

Unfortunately, Dr. Andersen's career was cut short by her death at age sixty-one. The cigarettes that were always dangling from the corner of her mouth were the most likely cause. In 1962, she was diagnosed with lung cancer. She underwent an operation, but the cancer was too far advanced. She died on March 3, 1963, in New York City.

The final chapter in the course of cystic fibrosis was written in 1989, when researchers found the gene responsible for the thick mucus. This gene regulates the passage of salt in and out of the cells. The discovery held out the promise that cystic fibrosis may one day be cured through gene therapy.

Jane C. Wright

Cancer Researcher

1919–

ew diseases strike such fear in the hearts of young and old alike as cancer. It is an ancient disease. Archaeologists know that cancerous tumors were observed by Egyptian doctors as far back as 1600 B.C., but the ancient Egyptians had no idea what those tumors were. As recently as the 1700s, doctors thought that cancer resulted from some type of peculiar inflammation. Then, during the 1800s, scientists developed the cell theory. They realized that the biological cell is the basic unit of all organisms, and that cells divide, creating new cells to replace those that die. By the late 1800s, they understood that cancer is the wild, uncontrolled growth of cells.

Effective treatment, however, was many years away. Since ancient times, surgeons had attempted to cut out cancerous tumors, but not until the 1930s and 1940s did powerful drugs become available that could kill cancerous cells. This type of treatment, called chemotherapy, was just being developed when Dr. Jane C. Wright began her medical career. She devoted her professional life to the study of powerful drugs and how they can be used to destroy cancers.

Jane Wright was born in New York City on November 30, 1919, into a family of prominent African-American doctors. Her father, Louis Tompkins Wright, was a distinguished surgeon and researcher, who established the Cancer Research Foundation at Harlem Hospital. He also was one of the first black Americans to graduate from Harvard Medical School. Louis Wright's father, Jane's grandfather, was among the first graduates of Meharry Medical College in Nashville, Tennessee. And a step-grandfather, William Penn, was the first black man to earn an M.D. degree from Yale Medical School.

Despite being born into such a rich medical tradition, there was no pressure on young Jane to become a doctor. She attended private elementary and secondary schools in New York City and was an outstanding student. In 1938, she won a four-year scholarship to Smith College. She loved to swim, and in college she set several records. She also developed a love of art and for a while considered becoming a painter. But in the end, she chose medicine.

After graduating from Smith in 1942, she was awarded a scholarship to New York Medical College, where she continued to be a brilliant student, and became vice president of her class and president of the honor society. After earning her M.D. degree in 1945, she served an internship and residency in internal medicine.

During this time, she met David D. Jones Jr., a recent graduate of Harvard Law School. They married in 1947 and raised two daughters while both parents worked in their professions.

After Dr. Wright completed her training, it was time to settle on a career. For six months in 1949, she worked as a New York City school physician and visiting physician at Harlem Hospital. She soon realized that she wanted to make a contribution to the treatment of cancer and joined her father's Cancer Research Foundation at Harlem Hospital.

The vivacious young doctor with the infectious laugh had found her life's work. She began to study how various powerful drugs and combinations of drugs affect different types of tumors. The idea behind all anticancer drugs was that they would kill off cells with particular types of characteristics. For example, some anticancer drugs attack cells that divide rapidly, a trait shared by all cancer cells. Some normal cells also divide rapidly, however, and so these drugs can produce undesirable side effects, such as nausea and hair loss, because cells that form hair and the lining of the digestive tract also divide rapidly.

Dr. Wright studied the effects of anticancer drugs on many types of cancer, including leukemia, breast cancer, melanoma, and cancers of the head and neck. Her work helped show that the most effective forms of chemotherapy usually involve combinations of drugs.

In 1952, Jane Wright's father died, and she took his place as the director of the Cancer Research Foundation. As her reputation grew, she was appointed to other important jobs. She became director of cancer chemotherapy research and instructor in research surgery at New York University Medical Center in 1955. She later became an associate professor. In 1967, she was named associate dean and professor of surgery at New York Medical College, where she set up a program to study cancer, heart disease, and stroke. Throughout those years, she also served on the staffs of several leading New York hospitals.

Dr. Wright also served as an adviser to agencies of the United States government. From 1964 to 1965, she was a member of the President's

Commission on Heart Disease, Cancer, and Stroke, and from 1966 to 1970 was a member of the National Advisory Cancer Council. She served on the board of trustees of Smith College and the American Cancer Society's New York division, on the editorial board of the *Journal of the National Medical Association,* and as vice president of the African Research Foundation.

For her contributions, Dr. Wright received many awards and honors, including honorary degrees from the Women's Medical College of Pennsylvania and Denison University. In 1987, Dr. Wright became professor emeritus and was free to pursue her other interests, such as sailing and painting with watercolors.

Elisabeth Kübler-Ross

◆

*Pioneer in the Care
of the Dying*

1926–

When Elisabeth Kübler-Ross was a young girl growing up in a rural village in Switzerland, she had her first encounters with the fact that people die. One of the most memorable occurred when a friend of her father fell out of a tree. He did not die immediately, but he was fatally injured. He called all the neighborhood children to his bedside to say goodbye. He was not afraid. He asked the children to help his wife and children run the farm. "My last visit with him filled me with great pride and joy," she recalled. His attitude helped young Elisabeth view death as a normal, natural occurrence. When she grew up, she became a psychiatrist. She devoted much of her career to teaching compassion for those who are dying and for their friends and families. She also made major discoveries about the emotional stages through which terminally ill people pass.

Elisabeth Kübler was born on July 8, 1926, near Zurich, Switzerland. Soon after she was born, she almost died. Elisabeth was one of a set of triplets and weighed only about two pounds (1 kilogram). Elisabeth was later told how her mother insisted on taking little Elisabeth home with her, rather than leave her tiny baby in the impersonal setting of a hospital.

When Elisabeth was in second grade, she again was faced with a death; this time, that of a young village girl who died of meningitis. The whole village mourned. "There was a feeling of solidarity, of common tragedy shared by a whole community," she later wrote in one of her books, *Death: The Final Stage of Growth*. "[The girl] was never removed from . . . her home. There was no impersonal hospital where she had to die in a strange environment. Everybody close to her was near her day and night."

Dr. Kübler-Ross contrasted this with her own experience in the hospital. When she was five years old, she was hospitalized with pneumonia. She was kept in isolation for weeks. When her parents came to visit, they were separated from her by a glass wall. "There was no familiar voice, touch, odor, not even a familiar toy," she recalled.

When Elisabeth Kübler became a teenager, World War II broke out in Europe. Switzerland remained neutral during the war and, as a result, thousands of refugees from Nazi Germany sought safety there. To help with the sick and injured refugees, Elisabeth worked as a volunteer at Zurich's largest hospital. After the war ended, she hitchhiked through European countries that had been ravaged by the war, even visiting a former Nazi concentration camp. She helped in any way she could. When she reached Poland, she helped two women doctors staff a small, poorly equipped clinic. That is when she decided that she would be a doctor.

She returned to Switzerland, enrolled at the University of Zurich, and earned her M.D. degree in 1957. While in school, she met an American medical student, Emanuel R. Ross, whom she married in 1958. They moved to the United States, and she became a citizen in 1961.

Dr. Kübler-Ross decided to specialize in psychiatry. After completing her medical and psychiatric training at hospitals in New York City and at the University of Colorado Medical School in Denver, she accepted a post in 1965 as assistant professor of psychiatry at the University of Chicago. Soon, she would be involved in the work that would make her famous.

It all began with a request by a group of students from the Chicago Theological Seminary, who asked her to help them do a study on death. Dr. Kübler-Ross suggested conversations with people who were dying. She and a hospital chaplain interviewed the patients while the students watched and listened behind a one-way glass window. Dr. Kübler-Ross found that the dying people were very willing to share their thoughts and feelings.

While talking with and counseling the patients, she identified five stages that terminally ill people pass through: denial, or the "not me" stage; anger, or the "why me" stage; bargaining, or the "why now" stage of trying to put off the inevitable; depression, in which the person grieves for himself or herself; and acceptance, the stage in which the dying person is ready to let go. Kübler-Ross wrote her conclusions in a now-famous book, *On Death and Dying,* published in 1969.

She then went on lecture tours, urging that courses be set up in schools and hospitals to teach people how to deal with death. She became especially concerned with the art of helping dying children. She recommended that parents let children deal with death early in life through such experiences as the death of a pet. She also became a powerful advocate of hospices, institutions that help terminally ill patients die with peace and dignity.

Kübler-Ross also worked in areas other than those dealing with death. She was acting and associate chief of the psychiatric inpatient service at the University of Chicago's Billings Hospital from 1965 to 1967. In the late 1960s and early 1970s, she served as a consultant to LaRabida Children's Hospital and the Chicago Lighthouse for the Blind.

A more controversial part of her research began in 1968, when she started to study the question of life after death. She interviewed people who had near-death experiences and, in 1975, made a public statement of her conclusion that there is life after death. She tried to prove scientifically that this is so, but her critics say she has failed to do so. Since then, Dr. Kübler-Ross has written several more books, given many lectures and workshops, and founded the Shanti Nilaya (Home of Peace) Growth and Health Center for teaching and therapy in Escondido, California.

For her tireless efforts on behalf of the dying, Dr. Kübler-Ross has received many awards and honors, including honorary doctorates from Smith College, the Medical College of Pennsylvania, Notre Dame, Loyola University, and many others. Her published works include *Questions and Answers on Death and Dying* (1972), *To Live until We Say Goodbye* (1978), *On Children and Death* (1985), *On Life after Death* (1991), and *Death Is of Vital Importance: On Life, Death, and Life after Death* (1994).

June Osborn

*Chaired the
National
Commission
on AIDS*

1937–

When news began to circulate about a mysterious disease killing young homosexual men in New York City and Los Angeles, few people suspected that this was the beginning of a new epidemic. But June Osborn did. "I remember the day the first report came out," she says, "June 5, 1981." The report described cases of a rare type of pneumonia in five young men in Los Angeles. The disease came to be called AIDS (acquired immunodeficiency syndrome). As a researcher on viruses and a government adviser on sexually transmitted diseases, it was soon obvious to Dr. Osborn that this was most likely a sexually transmitted disease. "We already were having a massive epidemic of sexually transmitted diseases," said Osborn. "So I knew that whatever AIDS was, it had a pretty fertile field to grow in." Other victims added to the list were people who had had blood transfusions. It was not long before the number of reported cases grew alarmingly, and June Osborn soon found herself playing a central role in the fight against this disease, as the chair of the National Commission on AIDS.

June Elaine Osborn was born into a family of intellectuals on May 28, 1937, in Endicott, New York. Both of her parents were professors at the University of Buffalo. Her father was a professor of psychiatry; her mother, of childhood education. In 1950, the family moved to Madison, Wisconsin, where her father became a professor at the University of Wisconsin and director of the Wisconsin state mental hygiene department. Her mother switched careers and became a psychiatric social worker.

Along with her older sister, June was encouraged to attend college and pursue an interesting career. It was the exception, not the rule, in the America of the 1950s, for women to have careers. Women were usually encouraged to stay home and become wives and mothers.

June studied chemistry at Oberlin College in Ohio, and, after graduating in 1957, decided to attend medical school at Case Western Reserve University in Cleveland. One of her mentors at Case was a Nobel Prize-winning virologist and pediatrician Frederick C. Robbins, who had made major contributions to understanding the virus that causes polio. He inspired June to become a pediatrician and a virologist.

Dr. Osborn received her M.D. degree in 1961 and then began training in her specialties. She spent three years as an intern and resident in pediatrics at Harvard University Hospitals in Boston, then went on to Johns Hopkins in Baltimore and the University of Pittsburgh School of

Medicine, where she conducted research on viruses. Her formal training completed, she returned to Madison in 1966 and become a professor of pediatrics and medical microbiology at the University of Wisconsin medical school. In 1975, she was appointed associate dean of the Graduate School. In 1984, she became a professor and dean of the School of Public Health at the University of Michigan. During this busy time, Dr. Osborn married and had three children—a boy and twin girls.

While still at the University of Wisconsin, Dr. Osborn began to be sought out as an expert to serve on government advisory panels. With her background as a virologist, she served as an adviser on vaccines (which protect against viral infections) to various government agencies, including the Food and Drug Administration and the National Institutes of Health. When medical researchers discovered that AIDS is caused by a virus that can be transmitted in blood and other body fluids, Dr. Osborn was called upon in 1984 to chair a working group struggling with the issue of AIDS and the nation's blood supply. All donated blood had to be screened for the virus, and Dr. Osborn helped draw up blood-testing guidelines that would also protect the privacy of blood donors. In 1985, she chaired a World Health Organization group dealing with the international blood supply. In 1989, she was selected to chair the National Commission on AIDS.

In this important new role, Dr. Osborn had to consider not only scientific matters, but also issues involving community interests and politics. Her honest, open manner enabled her to win the trust of groups as diverse as the radical ACT UP (AIDS Coalition To Unleash Power), and the Republican administration of President George Bush. From the time of her selection as chair until the commission was dissolved in 1993, Dr. Osborn watched as the pattern of the AIDS epidemic shifted from striking homosexual men, to intravenous drug abusers and heterosexual men, to women, and finally to children. In the absence of effective medicine to prevent or cure AIDS, Dr. Osborn stressed the importance of education about how AIDS is spread. Avoiding risky behaviors (such as unprotected sex and sharing intravenous drug needles) were at the top of her list of how to prevent AIDS. She also argued for the establishment of more drug treatment centers to help IV drug addicts kick the habit.

In 1993, with the work of the commission over, Dr. Osborn stepped down as dean of the public health school and concentrated on her teaching role as professor of epidemiology, pediatrics, and communicable diseases. In 1996, she became president of the Josiah Macy Jr. Foundation and moved to New York City

She received many honors for her work on AIDS, including honorary doctorates from Yale, Rutgers, and Emory universities, Oberlin College, and the Medical College of Pennsylvania (which began as the Female Medical College in 1850). She also was awarded the Scientific Freedom Award from the American Association for the Advancement of Science in 1994. Of all her accomplishments, Dr. Osborn is most proud of what did not happen with the AIDS epidemic—that it did not become as bad as it could have. "If we really believe this prevention stuff," she tells her friends in influential places, "we have to learn to celebrate things that don't happen."

Bernadine Healy

---

*First Woman
Director of the
National Institutes
of Health*

1944–

After seeing the movie *A Nun's Story,* about a Catholic nun who was also a medical missionary, young Bernadine Healy was reinforced in her desire to help people. She told her parents that she wanted to join a convent and become a nun. Her father, though a staunch Roman Catholic of Irish descent, was more realistic. He told her she never could be a nun because she would have to take orders from a priest, and she was not good at taking orders from anyone. She heeded her father's advice and, instead, satisfied her desire to help by becoming a doctor. But she did more than that. She became a leader in both private and public medical institutions and rose to become the first woman head of the U.S. National Institutes of Health.

Bernadine Patricia Healy was born in New York City on August 2, 1944. She was the second of four daughters in the family of Michael J.

and Violet Healy. The Healys ran a family business, selling perfume oils from the basement of their home in the New York borough of Queens.

The Healys believed that their daughters should have a good education. After World War II, girls usually were encouraged to become good wives and mothers, not career women. Both of Bernadine's parents had been raised by widowed mothers. They believed that women should marry and have children, but they also believed that young women should have a good education to prepare them for a practical career—just in case something happened to their husbands and they had to support themselves and their families.

So Bernadine was sent to a highly competitive public school for girls, Hunter High School, in New York City. She then won a scholarship to Vassar College in Poughkeepsie, New York, where she studied chemistry and philosophy, graduating with highest honors in 1965. She loved philosophy but wanted a more practical career. Medicine was a choice that satisfied Bernadine Healy, her mother, and her father.

When she began applying to medical schools, she ran into the obstacle of sexual discrimination for the first time. Although earlier in the 1900s there had been quite a few women in the medical profession, this situation had changed by the end of World War II. Men who had been soldiers flooded the schools and job market. Women were discouraged from pursuing most professions other than teaching and nursing. Healy was told that if she insisted on a career in medicine, she would be depriving a man of his place in medical school. Nevertheless, she was awarded a scholarship to the prestigious Harvard Medical School in Boston, one of ten women in a class of 120 students. She graduated with honors and her M.D. degree in 1970.

Dr. Healy then began the intensive training that would make her a leading cardiologist. First, she served an internship and residency at Johns Hopkins Hospital in Baltimore. Next she had a two-year fellowship in pathology at the National Heart, Lung, and Blood Institute. She returned to Johns Hopkins in 1974 as a cardiologist and served as a professor in the medical school from 1976 to 1984. Dr. Healy, a natural leader, radiated energy. She taught medical students, saw patients, conducted research, directed the Coronary Care Unit, and also served as an assistant dean for postdoctoral programs.

In 1984, Dr. Healy left Johns Hopkins for new challenges as presidential advisor, medical administrator, and high level policy- and decision-maker. She was appointed deputy director of the White House Office of Science and Technology Policy under President Ronald Reagan. In 1985, she became head of the Cleveland Clinic Foundation's research institute, directing nine departments, from cancer and cardiology to immunology and artificial organs. Dr. Healy served on government advisory panels and editorial boards of scientific journals.

As she progressed in her career, she created opportunities to bring change to an area that remains one of her greatest interests: women's health issues. Dr. Healy was particularly concerned about women and heart disease, the leading cause of death among older women. Too many of the major studies of heart disease had been conducted only on men. When elected president of the American Heart Association in 1988, she began one of the first studies on how heart disease specifically affects women. She wrote in the *New England Journal of Medicine* that the problem was to convince both doctors and patients that "coronary heart disease is also a woman's disease, not a man's disease in disguise."

A tremendous chance to support research on women's health came in 1991, President George Bush appointed Dr. Healy director of the National Institutes of Health (NIH). When she took on the job, the NIH, in her view, was "a sick patient." It had been without a director for almost two years. It was suffering from political interference, a drain of talented scientists, and a lack of funds. With typical energy, Dr. Healy set about curing the patient. She organized a plan to direct the use of NIH resources for biomedical research. She hired prominent scientists for leadership positions. She expanded the Human Genome Project for mapping the hundreds of thousands of genes that direct all workings of the human body. Perhaps most importantly for women, she set up the Women's Health Initiative, a $625-million, fifteen-year study of various factors that affect women's health. "The medical establishment had moved with glacial speed in responding to the unique needs of women," she announced. "I am here to attest that the Ice Age is over."

Dr. Healy ran into some powerful opposition within the NIH and in Congress. Controversy swirled over her handling of NIH researcher Robert Gallo and the claims of French scientists that Gallo had wrongly claimed credit for discovering the virus that causes AIDS. Dr. Healy insisted on proper medical procedures and due process in the investigation of such claims. (Dr. Gallo was fully cleared of these charges several years later.) She differed about gene patenting with biologist James Watson, the Nobel Prize-winning discoverer of the structure of DNA, the molecule of which genes are made. Watson resigned as head of the Human Genome Project. Through it all, Dr. Healy never feared taking a stand and speaking out. Observed one male colleague: "She acts swiftly and decisively, and some people get intimidated by that because she's a woman. When you get a guy who acts that way, it's leadership."

In June 1993, Dr. Healy stepped down as NIH director in the wake of Bill Clinton's election as U.S. president. Dr. Healy, a Republican, held views that were thought to be different from those of the new Democratic administration. She returned to her husband and two daughters in Cleveland and her work at the Cleveland Clinic Foundation. During this time, Dr. Healy directed the plans of the Page Center for new collaborations in areas such as managed care, and she completed her book, *A New Prescription for Women's Health: Getting the*

Best Medical Care in a Man's World.

She planned her book as a guide to what women should ask their doctors and to encourage them to ask these questions. In the book, Dr. Healy explains the ten main health problems that women may face in their lifetimes and provides information on their history, treatment, and research currently underway. She emphasizes the need for good nutrition and speaks honestly about such unique women's health issues as child-bearing, menopause, and osteoporosis. Dr. Healy wrote *A New Prescription* as a conversation between the reader and herself—as a doctor, but also as a woman, daughter, wife, and mother.

In January 1995, Dr. Healy became editor-in-chief of the *Journal of Women's Health.* Yet another new opportunity arose in 1995 when Dr. Healy was named to head The Ohio State University College of Medicine. Since her appointment as dean in September 1995, she has brought her typical intelligent leadership and energy into this excellent medical school. Dr. Healy has led efforts to develop a new School of Public Health at Ohio State, as well as new programs in molecular medicine, tumor genetics, and heart and lung research.

Dr. Healy regards herself as a feminist, and she has helped change how the medical profession views issues that involve women's health. She believes that past discrimination that prevented women from becoming doctors also had a bad effect on women's health in general. There were not enough women doctors to insist that more emphasis be placed on research into diseases that have special effects on women. Dr. Healy challenges the increasing numbers of women in the health-care professions to step out as leaders. She believes that only when more women are willing to take the "hot seat" in high-level administrative positions—as she has done—can there be a lasting improvement in the quality of women's health care.

Antonia Coello Novello

First Woman U.S. Surgeon General

1944–

Complications of a congenital illness plagued the childhood of Antonia Novello. She had been born with an abnormal colon, and had to be hospitalized for about two weeks every summer. She was eighteen years old before a surgical operation was performed to correct her birth defect. But her desire to help others who suffered as she had, and the example of the doctors who had helped her, inspired Novello to become a doctor herself. She became a pediatrician, then a government health-care adviser, and, finally, was appointed the first woman and the first Hispanic surgeon-general of the United States.

Antonia Coello was born on August 23, 1944, in Fajardo, Puerto Rico. When Antonia and her brother were young, their parents divorced. Her mother, a schoolteacher and later principal of a junior high school, took on the responsibility of raising the children. As a teacher, she understood that the road to success in life began with a good education, and she pushed her children to do well in school.

Meanwhile, Antonia, suffering with her colon disorder, began to have secret dreams of becoming a doctor for children. "I never told anyone that I wanted to be that," she later recalled. "It seemed too grand of a notion."

But with the support and encouragement of her mother, that grand notion became reality. Antonia enrolled as a premedical student at the University of Puerto Rico in Rio Piedras. She earned her B.S. degree in 1965, went on to the university's medical school in San Juan, and received an M.D. degree in 1970. That year, she also married Dr. Joe Novello, a U.S. Navy flight surgeon. The Novellos then moved to Ann Arbor, Michigan, where he specialized in child psychiatry, and she began an internship and residency in pediatrics at the University of Michigan Medical Center.

The sight of a woman doctor on a hospital ward was not a common one in the early 1970s. But her warm personality and professional competence saw her through any difficult times. In 1971, she became the first woman to be named Intern of the Year by the University of Michigan's pediatrics department.

Then, personal experience with illness once again inspired her career choice. Dr. Novello's favorite aunt died of kidney failure at the age of thirty-two. Dr. Novello became interested in kidney disease. She promised herself that nobody in her family would ever again "fall through a crack" in the health care system as her aunt had. She went on to specialize in childhood kidney disorders. After completing her training in Michigan and at Georgetown University, she joined the staff of Georgetown University Hospital in Washington, D.C. One year later, she joined a private practice of pediatrics in Springfield, Virginia.

In 1978, Dr. Novello decided it was time to leave private practice. She had seen too many cases that, as a private physician, she was powerless to help. She recalled many days when she monitored young patients waiting to be helped by the health care system, and was dismayed at how many slipped through the cracks of hospital and government rules and regulations. She decided that by entering government service, she could make a more significant contribution.

Since her husband was a navy doctor, she thought she might join the navy, but a male captain ended that idea at her job interview. "Didn't you hear?" he asked. "The navy's looking for a few good men." Dr. Novello then turned to the United States Public Health Service at the National Institutes of Health and was hired as a project officer for the artificial kidney program at the National Institute of Diabetes, Digestive and Kidney Diseases.

Dr. Novello made her greatest contributions in the field of public health. In 1982, she earned a master's degree in public health from Johns Hopkins University. Since then, her government career has prospered. In 1982 and 1983, she was a U.S. Congress fellow assigned to the Labor and Human Resources Committee. She had a large influence on drafting the National Organ Procurement and Transplantation Act of 1984. By 1986, she had become deputy director of the National Institute of Child Health and Human Development. In this position, she became especially interested in children with AIDS. Then, in 1989, President George Bush nominated her to became surgeon general, with a rank equivalent to vice admiral in the U.S. Navy. Congress confirmed her appointment in 1990, and she was sworn in on March 9, 1990, by another "first"—Sandra Day O'Connor, the first woman justice to sit on the U.S. Supreme Court.

As surgeon general, Dr. Novello gave special attention to issues pertaining to women and children. She was particularly active in the areas of teenage drinking, childhood vaccinations, AIDS, and cigarette smoking among the young. In 1992, she took on the powerful tobacco industry and singled out the cartoon character Joe Camel. The character was used to advertise Camel cigarettes, and it succeeded in encouraging smoking among young people. She also rallied against the powerful alcohol industry and their advertisements that contained misleading information about alcohol and youth.

After President Bill Clinton was inaugurated in 1993, Dr. Novello stepped down as surgeon general. She then turned her public health talents to the world stage and became the special representative to the Executive Director for health and nutrition at the United Nations Children's Fund (UNICEF). In this position, she continued to make important contributions to the health of children and women and served as a role model for both Hispanics and women. Dr. Novello is currently a visiting professor at the Johns Hopkins University School of Hygiene and Public Health.

Glossary

abolitionist
a person who worked to free slaves and end the practice of (or to abolish) slavery

AIDS (acquired immunodeficiency syndrome)
disease caused by infection with HIV, a virus that triggers a breakdown of the human immune system

alchemist
a person who practiced alchemy (the medieval science that sought to turn other metals into gold and sought a universal cure for disease)

alternative
a choice that is different from the mainstream or the normal; existing outside generally accepted beliefs

anatomy
the study of the structure of organisms and human beings; or, the body itself

anesthesia
the loss of sensation in a part of the body or in the entire body; commonly used in medicine to block the sensation of pain during an operation

anesthesiology
the branch of medical science that deals with anesthesia

anthropologist
a person who studies human beings, their history, and their relations with other races and their environment

antibiotics
substances used to kill disease-causing organisms in the body

antiseptic
clean and pure; free of the growth of microorganisms

appendectomy
surgery to remove the appendix

apprentice
a student who learns by working at a job with a more experienced worker

archaeologist
scientist who studies remains (such as artifacts and tools) of past human life and civilizations

atheist
a person who does not believe in God

autopsy
the medical examination of a dead body to determine the cause of death

bacteriology
the study of microscopic organisms

bacterium (bacteria)
single-celled microorganism that lives in soil, water, a plant, or an animal

benign
mild; kind; non-threatening to human life

birth control
medications or devices to prevent the conception or development of a fetus

blood transfusion
giving blood to a person who has lost blood due to injury, surgery, or illness

cancer
a type of disease in which certain cells in the body multiply in a disorderly fashion, become abnormal, and interfere with normal functions of an organ or body part

cardiologist
doctor whose specialty is the heart (or cardiology)

cardiopulmonary resuscitation (CPR)
procedure that restores normal breathing after cardiac arrest (a heart attack)

cardiovascular
relating to the heart and blood vessels

caste
social class in Hinduism

cervical cancer
a cancer that attacks the cervix (the entrance to the uterus in the female reproductive system)

charlatan
a fraud; a person who lies about or exaggerates his or her knowledge of a specific subject (usually medicine)

chartered
certified; officially established

chemotherapy
the use of very strong or toxic chemicals to treat cancer or other diseases

chloroform
a highly toxic liquid with an odor that can be used as an anesthetic

chromosome
a structure in cells that contain genes

colon
the part of the large intestine that extends from the small intestine to the rectum

congenital
physical or mental defect or disease that exists from birth

contraception
a method used to prevent pregnancy

curator
person who acquires and maintains objects in a museum

cystic fibrosis
genetic disease that causes abnormal amounts of mucus in the lungs and the digestive system

dehydration
condition in which a body lacks adequate levels of fluids

digitalis
drug used to treat heart conditions

diphtheria
dangerous bacterial throat infection

diuretic
drug that causes an increase in the flow of urine

DNA (deoxyribonucleic acid)
structure in living cells that contains the genetic material

dysentery
inflammation of the large intestine that produces abdominal pain and severe diarrhea, which can lead to dehydration

eclectic
a combination of many different beliefs or styles

electrocardiogram machine (or electrocardiograph)
a device that records the activities of the heart

embryology
branch of biology that deals with embryos (the earliest stages of a child's development in the womb)

encephalitis
disease that causes inflammation (swelling) of the brain

enema
injecting a fluid into the intestine via the rectum in order to clean the rectum

epidemiology
branch of medical science that deals with controlling disease in the population

fellowship
membership in an organization; or, money awarded to a member of a faculty

fetus
a developing, unborn baby from the third month of pregnancy until birth

gene
segment of DNA that carries traits inherited from parents

genetic
having to do with genes; physical trait or disorder inherited from previous generations

genetic engineering
altering the genetic material for an intended purpose (for instance, to cure a disease)

goiter
an enlargement of the thyroid gland, which is visible as a swelling on the front of the neck

gout
a disease marked by painful inflammation of the joints

gynecologist
a doctor who specializes in gynecology

gynecology
medical specialty that deals with female reproductive health

herpes
common viral infection that may affect the eyes, lips, fingers, or genitals

holistic medicine
treatment based on the complete person, not just the diseased part of the body

homeopathy
treatment in which very small amounts of medications are given to produce symptoms similar to, but much milder than, those affecting the patient

hormone
chemical substances produced in the body by endocrine glands and discharged into the bloodstream, which carries them to various organs that need them to function properly

hygiene
clean conditions that lead to good health

immune
biologically protected from a certain disease

immunization
the process of protecting a person against various diseases by injecting small amounts of the infectious agent into the body

impetigo
skin infection most often found in babies and small children

inflammation
a reaction by body tissues to damage or infection in which the tissue becomes red, swollen, hot, and painful

insulin
hormone produced by the pancreas gland that is essential in the body's regulation of carbohydrates; a person whose body does not produce enough insulin may develop diabetes

leukemia
type of cancer of the blood that causes it to produce abnormal white blood cells

lobby
to visit legislators in an attempt to influence their votes

louse (lice)
small, wingless insect that lives on (and feeds off of) other animals or plants

malaria
infection most commonly found in tropical areas that is transmitted to humans by mosquitoes

malignant
describes a dangerous condition, such as cancer

malnutrition
lack of adequate nourishment

meningitis
infection most commonly caused by bacteria or viruses that attack membranes, called the meninges, that cover the brain and spinal cord

menstruation
the monthly discharge from the vagina of blood and uterine tissues, along with an unfertilized egg

metastasize
to spread abnormal cells from one part of the body to another, thereby spreading a disease (such as cancer)

midwife
person who assists in childbirth

nervous system
the bodily system that is made up of the brain, spinal cord, and nerve cells

neurology
the study of the nervous system

obstetrician
doctor who specializes in obstetrics, or childbirth

opium
narcotic drug derived from the opium poppy plant

osteoporosis
condition in which bones become weak and fragile; most often affects older women

Pap smear
test that detects certain infections and cancer of the female reproductive system

pathology
the study of diseases and of their effects on the body

physiology
branch of biology that deals with the functions of life or living matter (organs, tissues, cells, etc.)

polio (poliomyelitis)
viral disease that affects the muscles and can result in permanent disability or deformity

professor emeritus
university teacher who has retired from active teaching but who is honored by keeping his or her rank

psychiatry
branch of medicine that deals with mental, emotional, or behavioral disorders

psychoanalysis
method of treating emotional disorders in which the patient is encouraged to talk freely about personal experiences (especially about early childhood)

psychology
science of the mind and behavior

psychosomatic illness
physical illness or symptom that is caused by mental or emotional disturbances

psychotherapy
treatment given to a person who has an emotional disorder (psychoanalysis is one kind of psychotherapy)

pus
yellow-white fluid that forms in infected body tissues

rectum
the lowest portion of the intestine

residence
period of active, full-time study at a university or hospital

rheumatic fever
disease that occurs mostly in children and young adults that results in fever, inflammation and pain around the joints, and inflammation of the lining of the heart and valves

scarlet fever
disease marked by a red rash and inflammation of the nose, throat, and mouth

sectarian
relating to a limited population or set of beliefs (or a sect)

sexuality
awareness of one's sexual feelings

sexually transmitted disease (STD)
infection (such as syphilis or gonorrhea) spread to a partner through sexual activity (formerly called "venereal disease," or "VD")

sterile
clean and free of living organisms and microorganisms

streptococcus; strep
bacteria that may cause a variety of serious infections, including strep throat

stroke
sudden loss of consciousness caused by a break or clot in an artery in the brain

suffragette
woman who fought for women's right to vote

suture
a strand of fiber used to sew up a wound or surgical incision in the body

synthesize
to combine two or more chemical substances to create a wholly new material

teething
the natural process by which babies grow teeth

temperance movement
political movement that sought to ban the use of alcohol

terminally ill
condition in which a patient will surely die from his or her ailment(s)

tetanus (lockjaw)
infection in which severe muscle spasms and seizures may lead to death; caused by the tetanus germ entering the body usually through a cut or scrape

tonsillectomy
operation in which the tonsils are removed because they have been infected with bacteria or viruses

tonsils
two glands located behind the tongue at the back of the throat

tuberculosis (TB)
infectious disease affecting the lungs marked by severe fatigue, weight loss, fever, coughing, and chest pain

typhus
disease often transmitted to humans by body lice that results in high fever, stupor, delirium, intense headaches, and a dark red rash

uterine tissue
substance attached to the walls of the uterus

uterus
the womb; the organ in the female mammal where a fetus grows and develops before birth

vaccine
a solution taken by a healthy person to protect the body against various diseases; the vaccine consists of whole or fragments of killed or weakened microorganisms that cause the disease

virologist
doctor who specializes in the study and treatment of viruses

virus
tiny infectious agent that grows and multiplies in living tissues and can cause various contagious diseases

yellow fever
disease caused by a virus transmitted by a mosquito

To Find Out More

Listed below are books, organizations, and web sites that provide more information on some of the people and issues described in this book.

Books

Alvin, Virginia and Robert Silverstein. *Cystic Fibrosis*. Franklin Watts, 1994.

Baker, Rachel. *The First Woman Doctor*. Scholastic, 1987.

Baldwin, Joyce Y. *To Heal the Heart of a Child: Helen Taussig, M.D.* Walker & Co., 1992.

Benson, Michael. *Coping with Birth Control*. Rosen Group, 1992.

Brown, Jordan. *Elizabeth Blackwell*. Chelsea House, 1989.

Cullen-Dupont, Kathryn. *Elizabeth Cady Stanton & Women's Liberty*. Facts on File, 1992.

Dubowski, Cathy E. *Clara Barton: Healing the Wounds*. Silver Burdett, 1990.

Epstein, Vivian S. *History of Women in Science for Young People*. V.S. Epstein, 1994.

Ferris, Jeri. *Native American Doctor: The Story of Susan LaFlesche Picotte*. Carolrhoda Books, 1991.

Ford, Michael T. *One Hundred and One Questions and Answers about AIDS: A Guide for Young People*. Macmillan, 1992.

Garza, Hedda. *Women in Medicine*. Franklin Watts, 1994.

Greenberg, Lorna. *AIDS: How It Works in the Body*. Franklin Watts, 1992.

Harvey, Miles. *Women's Voting Rights*. Children's Press, 1996.

Isler, Charlotte and Alwyn T. Cohall. *The Watts Teen Health Dictionary*. Franklin Watts, 1996.

Kay, Judith. *The Life of Florence Sabin*. TFC Books, 1993.

Knox, Jean. *Death & Dying*. Chelsea House, 1989.

May, Elaine T. *Young Oxford History of Women in the United States*. Oxford University Press, 1993.

Pollard, Michael. *Maria Montessori: The Italian Doctor Who Revolutionized Education for Young Children*. Gareth Stevens, 1990.

Rappaport, Doreen (Editorial Director). *American Women: Their Lives in Their Words*. HarperCollins, 1990.

Schleichert, Elizabeth. *The Life of Dorothea Lynde Dix*. TFC Books, 1991.

Shore, Donna and Giani Renna. *Nightingale*. Silver Burdett, 1990.

Standing, E. M. *Maria Montessori: Her Life & Work*. Dutton, 1989.

Stille, Darlene R. *Extraordinary Women Scientists*. Children's Press, 1995.

Whitelaw, Nancy. *Margaret Sanger: Every Child a Wanted Child*. Macmillan, 1994.

Online Sites and Organizations

American Red Cross
http://www.redcross.org/
Web site for the humanitarian medical organization founded by **Clara Barton** includes links to your local Red Cross chapter and a "virtual museum" tracing the history of the Red Cross.

American Women's Medical Association
http://www.amwa-doc.org/index.html
Leading association that serves the needs of women in medical professions and women's medical issues, founded by **Bertha Van Hoosen.**

Celebrating Women's Achievements
http://www.nlc-bnc.ca/digiproj/women/ewomen.htm
Online exhibit by the National Library of Canada focusing on several Canadian women of achievement, including **Emily Jennings Stowe.**

Clara Barton National Historic Site
5801 Oxford Road, Glen Echo, MD 20812
http://www.nps.gov/clba
The thirty-eight-room home of the founder of the American Red Cross.

Cystic Fibrosis Foundation
http://www.cff.org/
Organization that conducts research and helps treat patients with cystic fibrosis, the condition that was recognized as a disease by **Dorothy Hansine Anderson.**

Distinguished Women of Past and Present
http://www.netsrq.com/~dbois/index.html
Web site containing biographies of dozens of women in history, including several of
those described in this book.

Margaret Sanger Center International
26 Bleecker Street
New York, NY 10012-2413
http://www.interaction.org/mb/msci.html
Organization whose mission is to ensure that all people have the information and
services needed to manage their reproductive health.

Mayo Clinic
200 First St. S.W.
Rochester, MN 55905
http://www.mayo.edu/
The leading medical clinic in the country, whose history is linked to **Sister Mary
Joseph Dempsey**, head of St. Mary's Hospital in Rochester, Minnesota.

The Montessori Foundation
http://www.montessori.org/
Complete information about the education method founded by **Maria Montessori**,
including links to Montessori resources worldwide, biographical information about
Maria Montessori, and samples of her writings.

National Institutes of Health
http://www.nih.gov/
Web site for the federal government medical research organization formerly headed
by **Bernadine Healy**.

The National Women's History Project
7738 Bell Road
Windsor, CA 95492
http://www.nwhp.org/
Organization focusing on the role of American women in social, scientific, political,
and cultural history.

Planned Parenthood Federation of America
http://www.igc.apc.org/ppfa/index.html
Home page for the world's oldest and largest family planning organization; includes
historical information about and photos of **Margaret Sanger**, founder of the
American birth control movement.

UNICEF
http://www.unicef.org/
Home page for the United Nations Children's Fund, the worldwide organization that supports children's rights and health. **Antonia Novello** is currently executive director for health and nutrition at UNICEF.

United States Postal Service
http://www.usps.gov/
Search the website to view and purchase commemorative stamps of **Virginia Apgar** and **Alice Hamilton.**

WHAM! (Women's Health Action & Mobilization)
http://www.echonyc.com/~wham/
Activist group that supports issues concerning women's health.

Women's History
http://www.thehistorynet.com/WomensHistory/
Online magazine focusing on women in American history; Volume II Number 1 features an article on women in medicine.

Yale School of Nursing
100 Church Street South
P.O. Box 9740
New Haven, Connecticut 06536-0740
http://info.med.yale.edu/nursing/welcome.html
University nursing school founded by **Annie W. Goodrich.**

Index

About the Author

Darlene R. Stille is a Chicago-based science writer and editor. Currently the executive editor of the *World Book Annuals,* Ms. Stille has traveled throughout the world, from the rainforests of Costa Rica and Thailand to the mountains of Tibet and along China's Yangtze River.

She has an extensive background in the sciences, first as a premed student and then as a science editor for more than twenty-five years. For Children's Press, she has written more than a dozen books on such topics as environmental hazards, transportation, and the human body systems. Ms. Stille is also the author of *Extraordinary Women Scientists,* a companion to this book in the Children's Press Extraordinary People series.

Ms. Stille belongs to the National Association of Science Writers and the American Association for the Advancement of Science. She helped found Women Employed, an organization devoted to the equal employment of women, and she was the first chairwoman of the Chicago-based organization from 1973 to 1976.